superdrive

The ultimate new business process for agencies and creative consultancies who wish to win without the pitch.

superdrive

The ultimate new business process for agencies and creative
consultancies who wish to win without the pitch.

By David Chassar-Hesketh

Published by SuperDrive Ltd

Printed in the United Kingdom

First Edition published 2012

ISBN 978-0-9571370-0-4

superdrive

The ultimate new business process for agencies and creative consultancies who wish to win without the pitch.

This book is dedicated to Elaine, Madeleine & Samuel Chassar-Hesketh – who allowed me the time to write this book. Thanks also to the friendly coffee shops of London, LA and San Francisco that became my mobile offices. It is also dedicated to my parents - who showed me the way.

Contents

Pitch like an entrepreneur. Not like an agency

Codify your genius. Don't just claim it

Lead client engagements. Never be led.

The way ahead

Part 1

Pitch like an entrepreneur.
Not like an agency.

Our industry bemoans the pitch.

But we're addicted to it.

We simply cannot resist the call to demonstrate our genius.

It's been called the beauty parade.

It has built a subservient relationship where the client has dictated the brief, the cash and the process.

Clients love it because its allowed them to control and commoditise us.

It has been this way for decades.

But things are about to change.

We now live in a hyperconnected world where the rate of marcom innovation is now travelling at the speed of light.

There are so many new answers.

Clients need them.

We have them.

So now we hold the ace cards.

Now have the ability to drive our businesses like true spirited entrepreneurs.

It's time to take control.

It's time to choose our destiny.

We're marketers not sales people

All marketers are taught that marketing is superior to selling. We see selling as a lower form of doing business. After all, if you produce the right products and 'market' them effectively, then they will sell themselves, right? This almost subconscious notion that 'selling' is a lower form of activity has meant agencies have always sought to avoid it by dressing the selling process up in briefs, pitches and RFPs.

In fact, most directors in agencies come from either a creative or strategic background and would never dream of getting involved in 'selling'. At board meetings we discuss new business activities with our 'new business' director rather than our 'sales' director. We attend credentials and chemistry meetings, but only if we are sure the client has a brief or an RFP in mind. After all, we're not attending a meeting to convince anyone of anything – that's just not how things are done around here.

We're addicted to the pitch

We bemoan the pitch process constantly. In fact, there's not a year goes by within our industry without a call to stop all this 'free' pitching. But because we're all ambitious, confident and inspiring individuals in the agency business, we like an audience. We like the thrill of the big reveal and the opportunity to demonstrate our genius to a potential client in a shoot out with our rivals. So the pitch carries on.

Where the powerbase lies

Clients are addicted to the pitch process too. It ensures they keep complete control of it. They chose the when, where, how and why and as agencies we just do what we're told. You may deny this, but hand-on-heart do you really think you're the one in control of the relationship? Do you really think you're an equal 'partner'?

Unless you really don't need the fee or if you're a well respected agency at the top of your game, the best you'll get is a 60/40 powerbase split in their favour. It's just a commercial fact – there are thousands of agencies out there all willing to take your business – and the client knows it.

The magic moment of creativity

Of course the powerbase isn't always with the client. The reality is, when a client just loves your work and you've presented some of the smartest thinking on the planet they just have to work with you. This is that magic moment when you know they want what you have and you hold all the aces. But, in the main, this shift of power in your favour is short lived and immediately diminishes as the relationship is established and contracts are drawn up.

But let's note that magic moment when they are inspired by your thinking and want to move ahead. That's the only time in the traditional agency/client relationship when you truly have the edge. It's a fleeting moment but it's one I'm sure we've all experienced.

The good news is the opportunity to create such moments of inspiration in a client are becoming more readily available – this is because marketers, in this new hyper connected world, are going to need more inspiration than ever before because the possible ideas open to them is limitless. Also, the opportunity for you to maintain that powerbase long term is also available because this new hyper connected world of business is reinventing itself almost daily. So a marketers need for inspiration and guidance from gurus is growing exponentially as business opportunities do the same.

The new world economy

The 'mass market' model served us all well for over 100 years and pr, ad, direct and design agencies thrived in it. Companies built factories and products and then had marketing sell them (by spending huge amounts on mass media). We had mass advertising, mass markets, economies of scale, oligopoly dynamics and average products and customers.

But now that paradigm has started to breakdown. The last decade has seen the digital, connected world finally become a reality and the dynamics in terms of how to do business shift from big and financially powerful is best to quick-minded and fleet of foot is superior.

Even the largest of corporations are now focused upon constant innovation and testing then exploiting their successful products & campaigns rather than simply throwing money at opportunity (note that even P&G with a multimillion pound budget and the ability to sustain losses for 6 years couldn't make 'innovation' work by just throwing money at their cosmetics project *Reflect*).

It's true that mass advertising and average products still exist. But successful mass market models are quickly becoming a rarity as niche specialisation takes a large slice of their market share. The long tail is now just a fact of life. In fact, the market value of the 'tail' is actually as much, if not more, than the so called mass market end of the curve. If you needed proof of this, the Diversified Agency Services Group (DAS) at Omnicom, which runs all the non advertising parts of the company, has seen its share of the group's turnover grow from 11% to nearly 60% in less than 15 years. The long tail is the new money – have no doubt.

Spend less, think smarter

As the mass marketing model disappears from view, marketers with both large and smaller niche brands have sought to find new marketing solutions to meet their changing business needs. The answer used to be obvious – spend a bucket of money, build a brand via sheer brute force and they'll come. Now that just won't wash. Marketers are realising they don't need to spend $000,000 on a PR launch. Rather, they can probably test launch a product or proposition and, for very little investment, they get instant market feedback – the new marketing models really are allowing companies to test, assess, amplify and push onwards with those that work.

Why marketers' need help

But here's the marketer's issue - what is that ultimate mix? What is the next model? What are the new trends? Things are changing so fast - social media was simply an effective way of keeping up with your friends until recently. Now it's accepted as part of mainstream brand activity by most marketers. Mobile is coming of age – but there's 1001 ways of utilising it and big questions such as why create an app for it or should we go native or web are being thrown at us daily. Which is the optimum business model, strategy or media mix for my brand? These are the questions marketers are constantly asking themselves – and they don't have all the answers. In fact, no one has all the answers because the rate of innovation is now travelling at the speed of light.

To quickly run through some of the dynamics marketers are now experiencing:

Marcoms Strategies have more options than ever before.
Marketing communications has become much more complicated and

the strategies and tactics required for success far less obvious. Only a decade ago, if 5 agencies pitched for the same piece of business, they would all present very similar media strategies - with the only differentiation between each being at the fringes. This has all changed – everything and anything is now possible.

Experimentation costs have fallen

The cost of marcoms experimentation has fallen. It used to be very expensive to test run concepts and ideas – in both time & money - but no longer. In fact, if you pause, you've normally missed the boat such is the speed of change.

Little Fear of Failure

It's also worth noting that the fear of failure is also falling through the floor. It's now OK to experiment in public, get things wrong and move on in an orderly fashion. There is a caveat here however – some corporations still like to launch things with a fanfare – this is the old 'mass media' way of doing things. But large fanfares mean damaging climb downs. The new paradigm dictates that you experiment quietly and observe whether or not the concept is gathering momentum. If it is then amplify it. If not, then gracefully withdraw.

Market Segmentation like Never Before

Mass markets are melting away. For example, pop music album sales have gone from a million copies per week globally to just 43,000 in twenty years (amazingly, the week before his death, Michael Jackson's Thriller Album was only selling 1000 copies per month). Contrast this with the flourishing market for smaller, niche independent labels and artists that cover every conceivable genre on the planet. Anderson's long tail theory is certainly alive and well in this and many other market sectors.

New Strategies are Welcome
Even the big guys are realising that, once a trend has established itself, it's better to find another stream to swim in because there are an infinite number of new options available. For example, Wal-Mart's HQ has a large banner in its reception area stating, "You cannot out Amazon, Amazon." So marcom personnel are looking for new avenues – constantly.

Digital is topic of the day in the Board Room
In the UK, Philip Green of the Arcadia Group announced he'll be closing hundreds of stores whilst at the same time alluding to particular online fashion retailers as being 'amateurs'. In reality I can only imagine he made such attacks in a mixture of frustration and envy as he sees his tried and trusted business model get ravaged by the onslaught of a hyperconnected, digital world. There is now no doubt – digital is on the agenda in every boardroom across the globe (especially Philip Green's).

Can Clients still write a relevant Brief?
It's worth pondering the dilemma a marketing department faces as they attempt to write a brief that asks – we want the next big idea! In fact, if you think clients should be writing prescriptive briefs, and totally controlling the pitch situation you're wrongly assuming they have all the answers to their market issues. In fact, in this new world of hyper-connectivity, there are no all-knowing entities. And clients are increasingly acknowledging this as they look for partners to assist in solving and exploiting the changing landscape.

Business problems not marketing briefs

I remember working with a business consultant who used to open up chemistry meetings by asking, *"What's your biggest single business issue?"* This demonstrated nicely the fact that business consultants are not afraid of writing their own terms of reference (the name they give to a brief or contract). They'll discuss a client's business issues and then identify those they believe they can help with.

On the other hand, agencies have traditionally not been interested in business problems (they have always claimed to be but the reality is they've sold creative concepts and media strategies – full stop). And they were commercially right to do so in the past – this was where the immediate money lay and they hadn't the ability to influence a business beyond a new website, brochure, brand repositioning campaign, launch, et al.

But things have changed. Now marcoms holds many of the answers to the issues boardroom personnel are discussing. Agencies that get this (and are moving up their clients' value chains) are discussing business issues that can now be solved via marcoms. Liberating isn't it? The end of the finance era and the beginning of the marcoms era.

So the reality is marketers are looking for what I call the magic three i's;

Innovation – new ideas

Inspiration – new relevant ideas

Ignition – new ideas implemented

Marketers' doors have never been more open to new ideas than they are now. They positively need gurus and guides in this brave new hyper-connected world they find themselves in. Some are motivated by fear (how can I keep up with all this new stuff?) and some are motivated by greed (which is the next big trend I should exploit?). Either way, this need is ours to satisfy.

Briefs are commercially sound (not)

But as agencies we're still sat waiting for a brief, an RFP or word that they'd like us to pitch to them. They control the process. They control the when, where and how whilst we continue to tell ourselves this is the commercially sound way of doing things. After all, a brief shows commitment that they have a budget and a focus on what needs doing.

But the reality is not quite so commercially sound. As we all know, large, mass marketing budgets are disappearing in favour of smaller, niche based tactics, so the pitch that costs tens of thousands is becoming a thing of the past (or should be if you'd like to remain profitable – you just cannot justify such spend when the overall budget may not be more than tens or the lower hundreds of thousands in fees).

We've also all experienced the abuse the pitch process receives from clients – appointing no agency, having the budget halved or pulled, changing the terms of reference last minute, moving the deadline pitch date forward then taking 6 months over making a decision. We know them all. It really does become difficult to recognise what 'success' means. Even when we 'win' we're often not sure what it is we've 'won'.

But what is the alternative? I hear you scream. If we're honest, should we blame the client for acting in this way? After all, would you commit to something you've not seen if you could avoid it? The reality is

99.99% of us wouldn't pay in advance either given the chance. You'd want to know exactly what it was you were buying. And the counter argument that we've done fantastic work for others so they need not be concerned doesn't wash because you may not do great work for me. After all, we're talking creative output here and that's just plain unpredictable.

Sorry for being so harsh – remember – I'm in the same business as you and on your side. But I think its best just to tell it how it is. It's tough. Life's a pitch. We're used to it. But we will be fighting back – I promise.

Marketers' are like fish

There is an exception to the above – and that's the darling agencies that tend to win all the awards. A few manage to stay at the top of this tree for decades (an amazing feat and hats off to agencies such as AMV). But many rise from nothing, win awards, get on every pitch list (and normally win them) for around 2 to 3 years and then fade back into the agency supply haze. The truth is these agencies are not normally any better than the others they compete against. It's just they strike lucky and become a marketers new prey. Yes, marketers actually start to hunt them down. And to keep the nature metaphors coming, marketers are like fish – they swim in shoals - so once some of the larger fish decide to swim one way the rest follow.

Being the marketers' darling agency really is a great place to be. And you should strive to climb to this summit the whole of your career – but don't rely on it. It's a fickle business and there really are other, more sound ways now available of working with dream clients on your own terms.

The shifting powerbase

We've outlined the fact that, in the past, the powerbase between client and agency has certainly been in favour of the client. But I think this is about to change forever. As we've seen, marketers are increasingly aware that their business models need constant revitalisation and that the marcoms decisions they are making are becoming more complicated. In order to solve these challenges they are constantly seeking external insight. They are constantly looking for that new spark or a sense of direction. They realise that, more often than not, powerful ideas that drive business forward don't necessarily come from prolonged formal pitch scenarios.

They look at 3.0 agencies (those that just get the 21st century) and see that these agencies are now constructing products that their businesses can utilise - that the 3.0 tribe of agencies can create apps, develop content, build new media channels, find a new buying or communications process, et al. And they realise they need these ideas.

And it's not just the digital or large networks doing this. Even small design agencies are coming to the board room table with ideas that rock the way business is done. For example, by radically changing the way annual reports and corporate statements are taken to market - live conferences, video formats, digital dissemination to all key stakeholders, instant stakeholder feedback, the need for authentic stories to be disseminated to the market, the ability to provide corporate snapshots that count in a world of extremely short attention spans, the ability to gain attention in amongst all the clutter – it's all changing the way corporations communicate and do business with the city, investors and various other stakeholders. The medium isn't just the message any longer – the medium is now the driver of new business models.

So the marcoms industry is certainly a more exciting and less predictable place than it was a decade ago. Agencies now create ideas far beyond mere graphics, copy or plain obvious media plans. Rather, their ideas and product solutions are now only limited by their imagination. Anything goes. So it really is now the age of the idea.

Enter the entrepreneurial age

The age of ideas, new routes to market, media driven business models – it certainly looks like an entrepreneurial approach to marcoms is starting to emerge. Yes, the term 'entrepreneurial' has been bandied about for decades – but it was simply a platitude. 'We have an entrepreneurial approach to looking at your marcoms challenges' was a phrase we all loved to hate. It sounded clichéd and frankly it was.

But entrepreneurial, in the true sense of the word, we (as agencies) are becoming. We are now, more often than not, ignoring prescriptive briefs and instead becoming involved in shaping clients businesses. Even a web based landing page idea can now radically change the income flow of a business in ways that were simply just not possible a decade ago. Such is the power of marcoms 3.0.

Entrepreneurial we have become - either because the client is demanding it or because we have realised the client requires it. We are discovering we're best placed to develop new entrepreneurial ideas that can assist clients channel their business activity both to and from the market.

The right mindset

And we've the right psychological makeup to be true entrepreneurs. They say successful entrepreneurs have to be willing to invest and take calculated risks – agencies invest time and money in ideas constantly and are used to the 'winner takes all' reality of the commercial world.

It is also said that entrepreneurs have charisma, vision and the ability to take people with them on a journey. They have direction and know where they are going. They can inspire others. The type of entrepreneur I'm thinking of here would be Richard Branson - his legendary charisma and ability to inspire, his ability to see an opportunity where others are blind and then leverage it to the full – this is the definition of a true entrepreneur.

Pitch like an entrepreneur

Agencies have these entrepreneurial skills in buckets. So why do they insist on being subservient to clients? Consider Richard Branson and his approach to driving his business. Imagine how he would 'pitch' to potential investors or partners. Firstly we could certainly say that the entrepreneurial pitch is quite a different animal to the creative agency pitch. An entrepreneur would not sit back and wait for an RFP or an invitation to tender. They would seek out, find and make contact with the most ideal partners for their new idea.

It would be the entrepreneur who would decide the who, what, where, when and how of the pitch scenario. The marketing agency would seek permission to tender. The entrepreneur would seek out ideal clients / partners and aim to inspire and ignite a win/win relationship and move forward.

The entrepreneur would only seek out perfect partners – could you imagine Richard Branson getting on the phone and calling a couple of hundred potential investors asking them if they had any ideas for him to work on? It would be ridiculous. It simply wouldn't happen. He would call and state he had a proposition for them. He would dictate the who, when, what and how of the approach.

So there it is;

Entrepreneurs take control of the pitch process – the who, what, why, when and how they do business

Agencies are controlled by the pitch process – the who, what, when and how they do business is decided by the client

Notice the difference between these two types of pitch - the entrepreneurial approach allows for control and a mutual respect between parties. The agency approach means all the control and respect remains with the client. Now ask yourself, which of the two sounds more appealing? Pretty obvious really isn't it?

Taking your agency to market

More than ever you can develop ideas, methodologies, proven processes, media strategies and principles that are unique. In entrepreneurial mode, you can then identify ideal partners for said products and control how you approach them.

So why not change the paradigm? There's never been a better time in marcoms history. It really is time to start pitching like an entrepreneur and not like an agency. It's time to take control of your business. It's time to take your unique intellectual property to market.

As an entrepreneur, what have you got to pitch with?

So how do entrepreneurs pitch? Well firstly they'll look at the market and look for opportunities. They'll stick close to areas they understand and know well. They'll ensure their strategies are 'asset led' - that they have the skills required at hand (either within the business or hired in cost effectively) to meet identified opportunities.

Entrepreneurs run through the classic sales stages just like any other corporate sales process. The process is;

Discover – what the market requires

Devise – create a unique solution to these requirements

Deliver – take the product to market, building success upon success

It's exactly the same process for an agency - discover what the market requires, create a unique solution for that requirement and take that solution to the market. Sounds simple doesn't it? And it is if you can break the agency habit and start thinking like an entrepreneur. It's a completely different mindset. It will feel alien to start with but the rewards are immense and have the ability to allow you to take control of your agency's destiny like never before. Below are a number of useful principles that will help in framing an entrepreneurial approach to your new business strategy;

Go where the money is

Stay in markets you understand and are close to

Stay in markets where you can exploit existing company assets (intellectual, physical and capital)

Plan strategies that minimise risk and cash burn rate

Be prepared to fail early (in order to ultimately succeed as quickly as possible)

Create a proposition that allows you to enter the market with ease

Create a proposition that allows for differentiation and therefore margin protection (minimise the possibility of legitimate competition)

Go where the present and near future zeitgeist is because there is always more interest and growth

Utilise innovation carefully (realise it gains interest at the front end of the sales cycle but often is harder to close – the client just sees risk)

Go where you have conviction, the heart to see things through, a depth of knowledge and an obsession in the subject not found in your competitors

See speed to (or out of) market as a major competitive advantage

Do not waste time targeting the wrong partners or client base (focus upon the most important segments / clients and pursue them at all costs)

Always control the who, when, what, and how decisions of new business

Why clients think all agencies look the same

The reality is you'll have done some smart work at your agency. And you've probably created an amazing showreel or set of case studies that you believe will knock potential clients dead. The reality is – everyone does the above. I bet your showreel is less than 15 minutes long and follows all the rules. Ask clients if they watch show reels. They don't. I expect your case studies have three sub headings; background, what we did, the results. Sound familiar? It's no wonder agencies have become commoditised by clients. After all, who needs another 'me too' agency?

Go take a look at the websites of the top 100 agencies anywhere on the planet – 99.99% of them will have the following headers (or thereabouts); home, about, people, clients, news, services, contact. Sound familiar?

The sad fact is however – nearly all of these so called 'commoditised' agencies are anything but. In fact, it never ceases to amaze me the unique skills that lie hidden within an agency. No two agencies are alike. A particular agency is built on the experiences and knowledge of the people who work within it and the culture, customs, reputation and approach it takes. Some are fresh and sporadic. Some are experienced and structured. Neither approach is right or wrong – each has its merits and USPs – but in ways that appeal to clients in different ways.

The problem is, that unique skill base is never that easy for a potential client to discover because there's just an amazing sea of agency choice out there and it all looks very much the same from the outside. Hence the requirement for formal pitches, RFPs, tenders and even agency selection agencies.

To make things even more challenging for the poor client, the choice is so vast (not just in terms of agencies but also the media, route to market, product embellishments, innovation, etc.). So imagine how difficult it gets for the marketer – not only does she have to try to wade through a sea of undifferentiated agencies – she often doesn't even know what she's looking for in the first place (this is one of the criticisms often made of clients by agencies. However, I believe it's up to agencies to demonstrate what it is the client needs just as often as it is for the client to tell the agency what they require). Prescriptive briefs or open-ended business challenges – they are both legitimate. Both can be wrong or right in a given situation.

So give clients a fighting chance to understand you a little more. Cut through the commodity trap by articulating your genius rather than just claiming it. Brand your approach, principles and processes. Allow clients to precisely understand exactly what it is you do and how you do it. It's what makes you unique. It's what sets you apart. And, implemented correctly, it's the most powerful new business tool you have as an entrepreneur.

In Summary;
Pitch as a entrepreneur. Not like an agency.

Codify your genius. Don't just claim it.

Lead client engagements. Never be led.

Part 2

Codify your genius.
Don't just claim it

You are unique.

You think differently from the crowd.

So why follow the rules?

Why should you have a generic website, show reel or credentials?

Clients like to think there are 1000's like you.

They think you are replaceable.

Prove them wrong.

Ensure they'll want you with every sinew in their body.

Be the most successful entrepreneur on the planet.

The one clients wish to invest in.

Discover your uniqueness.

Celebrate it.

Codify it.

And launch it to the world.

A need for differentiation

The truth is the 'uniqueness' of an agency is due to the way things are done rather than what is done, because all agencies offer, superficially, very similar services. But it's a sad fact that most agencies don't articulate what it is that makes them unique very effectively because they don't understand this distinction and carry on telling potential clients about what they do than rather than how they do it.

Agencies bang on about disciplines, market experience via case studies and their people but don't articulate the unique way in which they do stuff – so they remain commodities because every other agency is doing the same thing and the client is none the wiser.

Even worse, many agencies don't even realise what it is they do uniquely – they go about projects without being conscious of the mindset and models that allow them to produce the magic they do. The danger with this approach is three-fold - i) the client may not appreciate your genius because all they see is the end result, ii) if the people creating the magic walk out of your building tomorrow, would you know how to recreate it in their absence and iii) if you're expanding at a pace, how do you keep true to what made you successful in the first place if you cannot articulate effectively how things should be done to new members of the team?

The client's perspective

Place yourself in the mindset of a client by experiencing the commodity issue they face. Take a look at the top 100 agencies online in your country (or globally). Spend an hour and note what they claim about themselves. I bet they'll shout about their experience and their disciplines till the cows come home. They'll bang on about what they do, but not about how they do it. They will all, in the main, sound the same. And that is why homogenization is the norm.

Clients take agency discipline lists, case studies and relevant experience as a given – they are merely the essentials for entry into the game. Agencies act as though, by having these three essential hygiene factors, they should have the client on their knees with a brief. But the client sees things rather differently. What they are really interested in is how you do things because that provides them with an insight into what it would be like to work with you and how consistent you'd be at delivering great work. Remember, they are not interested in the fact you've done great work before – they're interested in whether or not you'll do great work for them!

Proprietary systems and models

Some agencies, in order to attempt to solve the homogenization issue, have created proprietary systems which they use to solve client problems. However, to create one is not enough. Even agencies with proprietary models often make the mistake of seeing them as merely a tool for client workshops. On the contrary, an agency proprietary model can be utilised in many ways;

It's a tangible product that the client can grasp hold of and understand immediately

It is an extremely effective repositioning tool (with or without having to rename the organisation)

It can be utilised within existing client relationships to add value and keep account teams more focused

It brings a new sense of focus within the agency

It allows you to build a knowledge and credibility in areas where you have expertise

It can bring focus to your social media strategy (such as your agency blog)

You can build up a track record of success

It becomes a code by which the agency lives

It's a new business tool for igniting new business relationships and running a sound engagement process

It adds a new $ value to the business (one that can outlive individuals within the business)

It creates a focused sales process

It can be modified to work in different sales situations

Constructing a proprietary system

I realise you'll have processes in place for traffic control, briefing, planning and billing. Although these processes are important to the running of the agency, they are not what we're interested in here. Rather, we're now focused upon codifying the 'magic' that lies within your agency into a set of coherent and tangible tools that can be taken to market.

This practice of creating proprietary systems in not new – it's just that many agencies have not realised the power of such a tool in the new 21st century economy.

As mentioned, famous examples of proprietary systems include;

TBWA with Disruption

Kunde and Co with Corporate Religion

Saatchi and Saatchi with Lovemarks

Brains on Fire with Brains on Fire (10 principles for WOM campaigns – I like the fact the name of the agency is also their app)

Ideo with Design Thinking

Each of the above has understood the power of codifying what it is that makes them magic into a coherent set of tangible tools. And the concept of 'tangible' is important here. You can literally get hold of a Disruption or Lovemarks model. They are proven so clients know what they are getting when they commission a Lovemarks, Corporate Religion, BOF, Design Thinking or Disruption assignment - they get focus and a proven robust approach. I'm not saying these agencies have got it right - and most are guilty of still using their proprietary systems merely for workshops. But nevertheless, each has experienced the power of a branded methodology in adding value to the client relationship.

It's my aim not only to run through the key stages of creating your own proprietary system but to also drive home how to fully utilise it to drive extraordinary new revenue growth.

The key components in a proprietary system

We wish to take the magic within your agency, brand it as a system and take it to market. It really is that simple. To this end we need to collect information that creates that magic, codify it and then brand it so it will appeal to our target audience.

This information will consist of all the experience, history, wisdom, logic and inspiration that has been utilised successfully by the agency in the past. Where you place this in a physical sense doesn't really matter – it could be as simple as a folder on a server with a number of sub categories to organise information or it could be as sophisticated as some form of intranet system. I call this depository of information your agency's BrainBank. This is your knowledge base – the font of all shared knowledge.

Once you have started populating your BrainBank (and this should be an ongoing, continuous process), we need to take relevant elements from it and create products that we can take to market. I call these products 'apps' because the emphasis is on the application of such branded products (and they also normally consist of an *approach, process* and set of *principles* so it also works well as a mnemonic).

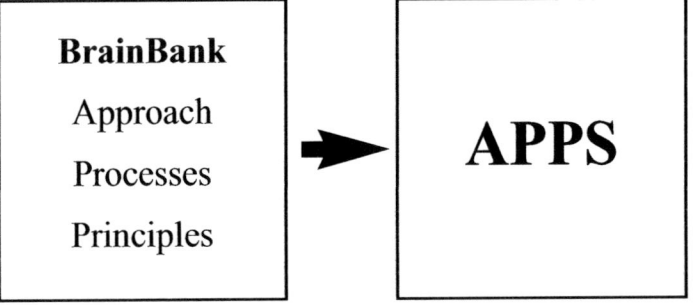

Figure 1: Constructing apps from your BrainBank

Constructing a BrainBank

I'll assume there is no central source of information and that the agency's approach, processes and principles have, in the main, been informal to date (excluding production and billing which I'll assume are in place!). To get started, below are some quick fire questions to gain an overview of the agency. You should interview all the key personnel within the agency in detail on a 1 to 1 basis (30-45 minutes should be enough per person) using these questions as a prompt sheet. All other personnel should receive an email questionnaire version.

Quick Fire Questions;

1. Elevator test – how would you sell this business in 30 seconds?
   It's amazing how these can differ from one team member to another.

2. What are the key drivers of the business in terms of the 7s's

   Situation Analysis – where are we now in terms of financials and client base?

   Strategy – where do we wish to be in terms of financials and client base? How we are getting there.

   Structure – what is the current structure of the organisation in terms of mgmt, brand, service delivery?

   Skills – disciplines, industry knowledge, experience, others

   Staff – who are the key drivers within the business? What do they do?

   Systems – what approaches, processes and principles are in place currently?

   Style – what is the culture - 'the way we do things around here'?

3. What constitutes the company's positioning strategy to date? Is there anything you would change?

4. Who is the ideal client?

5. What is your best work? From a planning and creative output perspective

6. Awards won – Who for? Which awards? Other endorsements (i.e. academic)

7. Market sectors – your top three given the choice / reasons for choice

8. What issues are your top three target market sectors facing that you could address?

9. Who do you admire as best practice? Other agencies / companies in other industries

10. Your commercial targets? Sales / GP – where does the income come from in terms of disciplines / clients?

11. How have you approached / found new business in the past? Breakdown by method

12. Breakdown of key stages in the briefing process

13. Breakdown of key stages in the account mgmt process

14. Information on existing processes and models utilised within the agency

The above will provide a sound backdrop. What follows are a number of tools you can utilise to drill deeper into the agency's skill base to further populate your BrainBank.

Further BrainBank data sources

Campaign value chain

Break down your campaign value chain into its constituent parts (you may develop a number of these depending upon your agency and its skill base). Then drill down at each stage to understand and codify how things are currently being done. Note those that are effective. Note the maverick, the common place. Use a 'creative pause' technique – by stopping at certain points and questioning how things are done and ask how they could be done better.

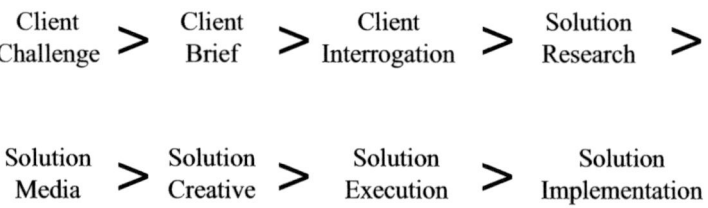

Figure 2: The campaign value chain

Disciplines

I call this the discipline wheel. It's a useful prompt when running through key discipline skills. Start by highlighting the key disciplines within the agency on the wheel. Then analyse and codify what's being done presently, note which are effective or maverick or common place. Use the creative pause technique and ask how things could be done better / best practice within the agency.

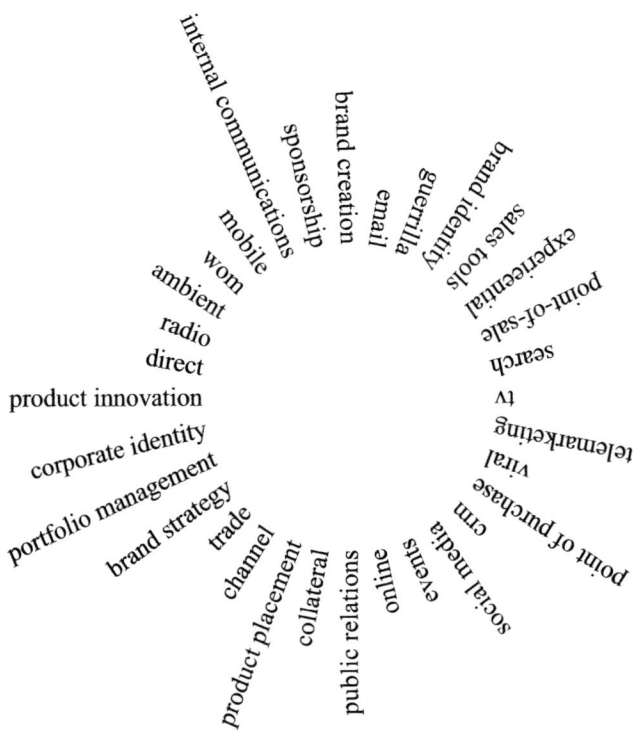

Figure 3: The discipline wheel

If you're looking to drive campaigns with discipline driven propositions, you'll be more effective if you lead with a hot topic as it can be an effective door opener. Mobile media during has is been an example of this – it sits at the innovation sweet spot but in terms of % of market spend it's still relatively small.

A useful model to keep in mind when considering which products to call innovative is the three circles of innovation model (there are so many versions of this I'm not sure who originally developed it) which visually allows you to place certain disciplines and client needs in one of three circles. The key insight is that new ideas work their way from circle three through to circle one if they are adopted by the market and become common place. The key is to identify those in circle three that look at though they are heading towards circle two.

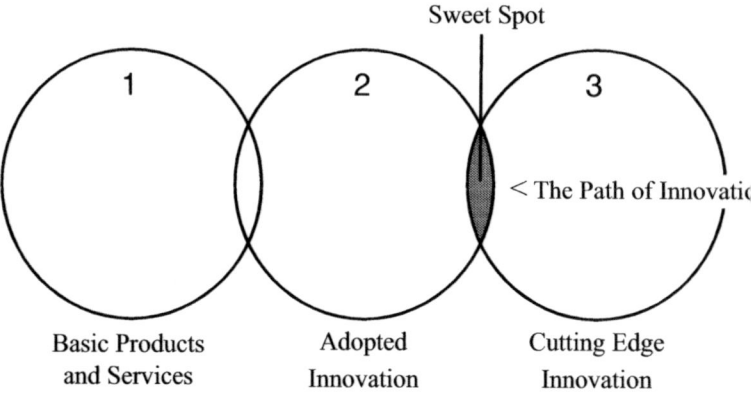

Figure 4: The three circles of innovation

Sector Driven

This is an agency favourite – and one where many mistakes are made. Ensure a chosen sector is large enough to warrant the effort required to launch a campaign to it and possibly allows you to recycle the knowledge gained across a number of clients in subsectors. For example, financial services will allow you to do this as it is a large market with many players and sub-segments, whereas the hotel sector may not because it's a very small market place with only a handful of key players.

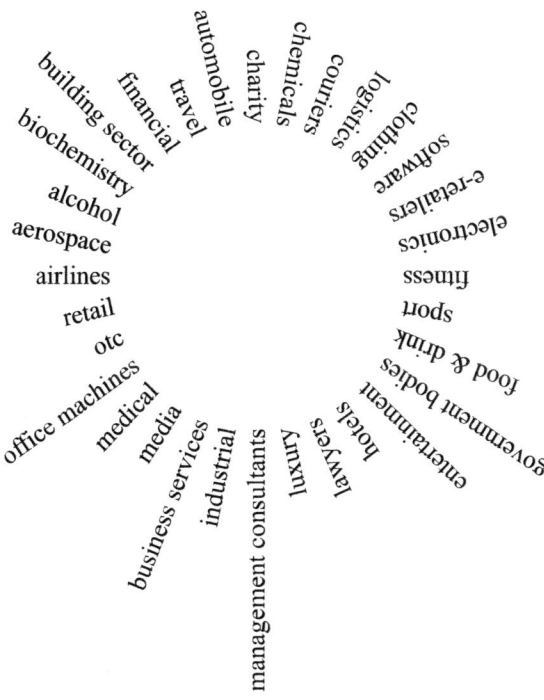

Figure 5: The wheel of macro markets

These can be broken down into subsegments:

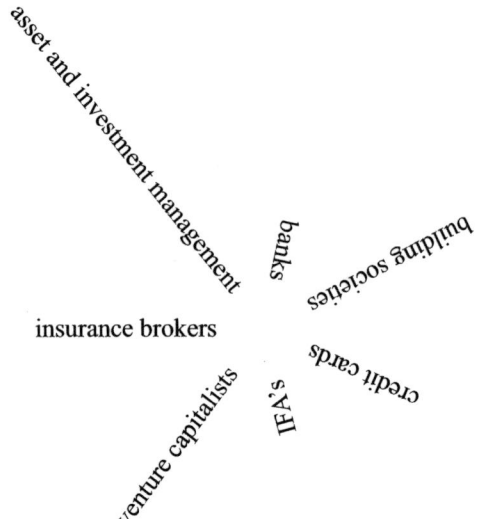

Figure 6: The financial market wheel

And then broken down again – take banks:

Figure 7: The banking market wheel

Issue Driven

The wheel would be so large I've not created one. Issues in business are a limitless goldmine. Issue driven tools are exciting because they can work across markets and therefore have huge potential. For example – if you have a proven set of principles for producing internal communication programmes that motivate the hell out of consumer facing staff then you can take this to many markets.

If on the other hand you've developed a proven set of principles that have driven campaigns in the insurance broker market then your options are limited (although you could change this skill via repositioning to be a set of principles that work in b2b sales environments to expand the concept – either within the finance sector or beyond).

The generalist / specialist mix

Attempt to develop principles that can be defined in generalist terms but then allow for a 10% addition for particular market places. The proposition works along the lines of, 'We have a proven set of principles that have solved X and we believe they are directly relevant to your given market conditions A, B and C

.

Where - X is a perennial issue across a number of markets but A, B and C are market conditions which ensure X is directly relevant to the potential client. Result – specialisation without limiting your agencies growth potential.

Constructing apps

Once you've completed the above you'll have a good overview of your agency and its skill base. The next stage is to create your app(s) – the branded products that we will take to market.

All the elements of your app should fit into one of the following categories;

Figure 8: The app

This is what each of these elements stand for in more detail;

Your approach – is often given no more than a page on your website and means different things to different agencies (normally full of platitudes such 'creative' and 'entrepreneurial'). I define your approach as being the "The beliefs and assumptions that drive your agency". Such beliefs and assumptions consist of your SWOT (strengths, weaknesses, opportunities and threats) and how you see these affecting your business. Matching your strengths and weaknesses to market opportunities has always been the everlasting, ever-changing challenge we face in business. But it's now even more challenging (or full of opportunity depending on how you feel about the twenty first century) due to the exponential growth in media options and the changing face of capitalism (see Umair Haque's The New Capitalist Manifesto for a fantastic run down on where capitalism in going this twenty first century).

Your processes – These are the chronological or iterative steps you structure a project by. Processes bring order. They drive work through to end goals. They allow for progress to be managed. They can assist in the creative process enormously by giving a focus and momentum to your work. Certain types of projects require a more chronological approach – many mgmt consultancy models and production processes offer examples of this. Others lend themselves well to the iterative approach – creative hothouse models or brainstorming activities are examples of this. I often think both types should be apparent in your agency – and it may be that both are used for the same project – often principles drive insight and process drive the project.

A note on processes and why they really are important (inspired by Seth Godin); A process is like a roadmap and human beings really need them. To illustrate the point; San Sauman of the Max Plant Institute for Biological Cybernetics, studied what happens to us when we have no map, no compass or any way of determining landmarks. He did this by studying what happens to people when they are lost in the desert. He found that, when they wanted to walk in a straight line to get out of the heat they ended up walking around in circles. It seems our instincts are not enough – human nature needs a map if it's to avoid walking in circles.

So the message is clear – a process will ensure you're effective and efficient.

Your Principles – By 'principles' I'm not considering morality (I'll assume this is in place already). Rather by 'principles' I mean the rules, insights and models used to generate client ideas. For example, TBWA's Disruption has many models within its toolkit to assist in idea generation – such as The Brand Wheel, The Connections Scenario, The Persuasion Sequence and The Ideas Impact Monitor. Other agencies have principles that are almost like dictates that they use to guide them through the ideas process. For example, Brains on Fire, a word-of-mouth consultancy in South Carolina, has developed 10 principles to live by if you're looking to create successful WOM movements both on and offline. They are not 'how to' models but rather guiding advice given with plenty of inspirational anecdotes.

The differing types of apps

You can adopt many different approaches to constructing an app. Here are some examples;

PROCESS DRIVEN
These apps take the client through the complete project. For example: Kunde and Co and their Corporate Religion approach which uses a chronological process (using a hurdle race as an analogy).

Another example is one I have used since my days in consultancy – 3D

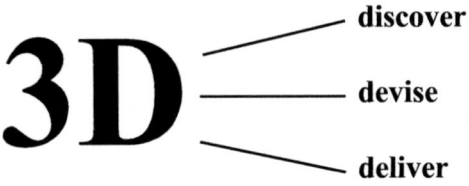

Figure 9: 3D

Each of the above walks the client through each of the stages of a project in a chronological order. 3D is a very powerful app that it very adaptable.

DISCIPLINE DRIVEN
This app takes the client through a particular discipline or aspect of a discipline. For example – Interbrand's three-stage model to brand evaluation.

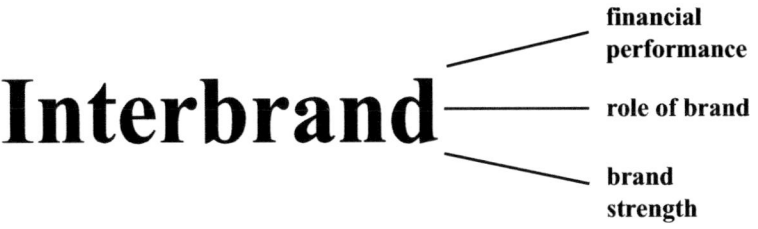

Figure 10: Interbrand's three-stage model

APPROACH DRIVEN
This allows the agency to be driven by a certain ethos. For example; TBWA and Disruption – where the notion of a 'Disruption' from the norm, in order to create new ideas, is the order of the day.

PRINCIPLES DRIVEN
This allows the agency to be driven by a set of principles or models – The Brains on Fire agency is a good example of this with their 10 principles of WOM campaigns.

Any of the 22 Immutable Laws and Marketing could also be deemed powerful principles (they really do stand up after all this time).

Developing tools - some examples

Here are some app examples I find really useful.

VENN'S
The good old Venn diagram – they are just so flexible and can be understood instantly. Here are two powerful examples;

Ideo are one of the new model agencies who assist organisations innovate and grow. Need I say more? The diagram says it all!

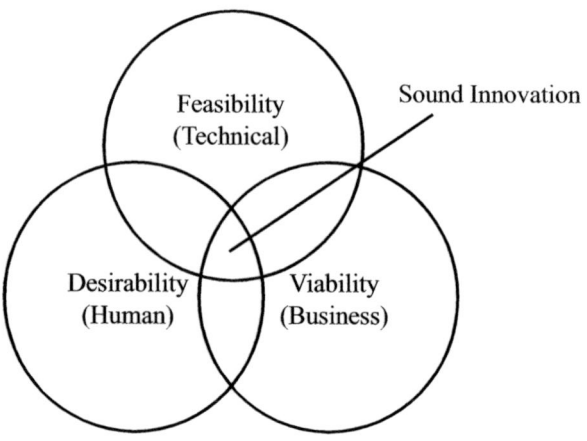

Figure 11: The Innovation Sweet Spot

ALIGNING YOUR BRAND PERSONALITY

This Venn diagram is based upon the work of Alfred Adler, a psychologist, who concluded that there were three constituent elements of the human personality and the more they harmonise, the stronger one's personality becomes. The three elements are:

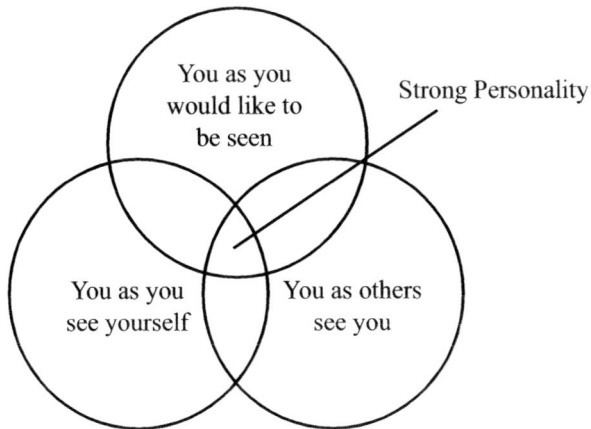

Figure 12: The 3 Dimensions of Personality

The 3 dimensions of perception works just about anywhere and is highly adaptable! It's great for brand personality work, social media planning or internal marketing campaigns for example. Anywhere it's important to align all stakeholder beliefs.

MECE (Mutually exclusive, collectively exhaustive)

A principle rather than a diagram used by McKinsey. The rule is – do not have multitudes of headings for a particular subject or topic unless each one is absolutely mutually exclusive from the others (if it's not exclusive then it should be under another heading). It really keeps things clean and tidy in your mind and forces you to focus on the key driving issues. Collectively exhaustive – stop when you've found all the headings (normally 3 is a good number).

RULE OF THREE

Another McKinsey principle which you just have to stick to or you're fired! Try to keep any list to no more than three things. Three reasons why we should do this, three factors that contribute to that, three reasons why this shouldn't be done. It keeps a momentum in the mind but it doesn't allow for irrelevant dribble. Nice one.

THE CASCADING RULE OF THREE

I developed this having been exposed to the rule of three above. OK – so you've got your 3 factors that are MECE. For each of these factors have another 3 sub-factors and so on. You can really drill down into a subject.

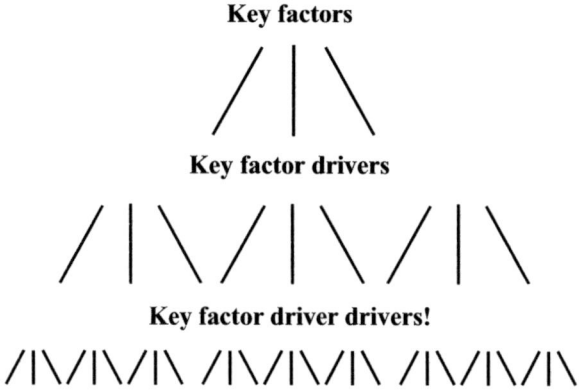

Figure 13: The cascading rule of three

This is a great way to construct the facts on a particular sector, subject or issue. Also a great way of starting to write a paper on a subject. You'll have all the key facts in front of you on one sheet and they'll all be neat and MECE (mutually exclusive, collectively exhaustive).

RETRO
This really is a powerful tool when it comes to reassuring a client that you've considered the logic behind a campaign from a commercial POV.

Basically, collect successful case studies, anecdotes, et al – from business, marketing or life in general as appropriate. Then deconstruct the logic that made the idea so successful. Apply this logic to a client's issues. Ergo – it worked for them and it will work for you to – they are proven principles.

GURU GUIDANCE
Find blogs, papers, writers and case studies – anything that inspires you - then log them in your BrainBank. It's amazing how they build up and become useful. I find people like Seth Godin (a great blog to register to) and Tom Peters (an ex McKinsey mind) just goldmines when it comes to inspiration. Find those that inspire you and adapt their concepts and ideas so they will work given your context.

BREAKEVEN
This is so simple it shouldn't really be here but it's amazing how many people forget this one if they are spending other people's money. It's not always appropriate but if it is you really better have thought about it because otherwise you're an art tart and not an entrepreneur!

$$\textbf{B/E} \;=\; \frac{\textbf{Cost of campaign}}{\textbf{GP margin}} \;=\; \textbf{B/E turnover}$$

$$\div \; \frac{\textbf{unit sales}}{\textbf{price}} \;=\; \textbf{Units to B/E}$$

Figure 14: Breakeven

An Aside – Make your apps so simple they can be understood in minutes and adapted easily. If your concepts are simple to understand people will adopt and adapt them quickly. If they are not they'll move on. The more of your models clients adopt and utilise within their business, the more you've a strong, long-lasting relationship built on credibility and trust. If you're looking for something a little more complex with data underpinning a simple model go for it – but my take is always use these to support your main presentation because most people use their gut when initially making a decision and then seek the numbers to simply justify their decision (The theory of 'Blink' by Malcolm Gladwell explains this decision making process brilliantly).

Utilising the app in the sales process

Principles are sexy, dynamic and they are ultimately what inspire the client at the front of the sales process. Processes on the other hand are more about surety of delivery and are often used at the closing stage of the process.

It is worth reminding ourselves that the reason we've created our apps in the first place is to win more business - to be successful in the engagement process with potential and existing clients. If you consider the power of apps in the sales process and utilise them appropriately they become a very powerful tool indeed. For example, consider the two senses of the word engage;

1. Engage – agreeing to a relationship. This sense is charged with emotional content and sentiment.
2. Engage – a mechanical process – It's like two ships in space engaging. Logical, mathematical & process driven.

In order to succeed in new business, you need to be 100% with the two senses of the word 'engage'. The emotional sense of the word should come through your principles. These are sexy and seductive. They open doors and grab peoples' attention. The mechanical sense comes through your processes. These are required when you're looking to close said client. At this point they are looking for reassurance and surety. The two senses of the word 'engage', when working in harmony together, creates a powerful new business closing strategy.

TBWA with Disruption, Kunde and Co with Corporate Religion, Saatchi and Saatchi with Lovemarks, Brains on Fire with Brains on Fire - each agency has understood the power of codifying what it is that makes their magic into a coherent set of tangible tools. And the concept of 'tangible' is important here. You can almost get hold of Disruption or Lovemarks. You know they are proven so you know what you're getting when you commission a Lovemarks, Corporate Religion or Disruption assignment. You get focus and a robust approach.

Yes, you still get creativity – said client doesn't for a moment think that such processes will stifle great creative work – they see great creative output as a given (and if genius insight is not forthcoming then no amount of process badge-making will keep a client engaged for long). But, assuming you've delivered the genius that knocks the client over, they'll go on purchase only if they're sure you can deliver it – appropriate apps can assist in this reassurance process.

What follows are some further observations regarding the utilisation of apps.

Proprietary tools and creativity

It is the propensity of 'creative types' to run a mile when they are asked to utilise a process. Surely it will kill creativity they scream. The reality is the proprietary process driven agency can set itself free to be even more creative than those that start with a blank sheet. Blank sheet agencies spend far too much time at the starting line wondering which way to go. Process driven agencies efficiently create roadmaps and therefore can spend more time actually considering how to creatively execute their solutions.

Strategically driven agencies will tend to utilise their proprietary tools as a chronological roadmap. Creatively driven hot shop agencies will tend to utilise their system to post rationalise their genius – both approaches work and often it's only in hindsight you'll know which one to emphasis given the challenge at hand.

Don't become product driven

Agencies sometimes make the mistake of developing ideas that are complete in their own right and then attempt to sell them to market. For example, they have a wonderful idea for a credit card concept so they hawk that idea around the key players within that industry (one agency did just this – a fantastic online concept. People were interested but no business was forthcoming). You may be lucky... but the chances of a potential client being in a position to be able to utilise that exact idea is near on zero.

Don't make the mistake of thinking your apps should have such specific product ideas within them. This certainly is not what I'm advocating. Rather, remember you have a set of proven models and principles that are able to solve challenges and bring light to opportunities that are directly relevant to the client. *You are seeking to understand their issues and then apply your app tools to those challenges.* Don't go creating a better mousetrap (with respect to Ralph Waldo Emerson). Wait to see what it is the client wants to catch and then utilise your apps to create a solution to that particular issue.

Note: This principle is changing as agencies create digital products of their own. But it's early (and exciting) days.

Utilising an app is like playing basketball

When creating models and principles, it's important to remember that they must be flexible enough to work in the real world in what will be a diverse plethora of marketing challenges. The best models are those that are simple to understand (in 30 seconds maximum) and have an open architecture so they can be used in as many different scenarios as possible. You should mentally imagine your principle sat in the middle with client challenges approaching it from any one of 360 degrees with you effortlessly being able to solve that challenge using one of your apps. I call this the art of pivoting (rather like basketball players do – they have a firm footing - your BrainBank or particular app - but are able to turn 360 degrees effortlessly).

The opened-minded state (example of app flexibility)

This model is based on the notion that most client briefs seek to change people's perceptions and therefore actions. Along the bottom of the triangle we see our objective – to move said audience from an existing perception to a new perception. However, we have not considered the fact that the recipient may not be all that easy to convince that their existing perceptions are wrong. In fact, as a rule, people don't like having their existing belief systems challenged and therefore they resist any approaches (hence the wall of prejudice we hit along the bottom of the triangle).

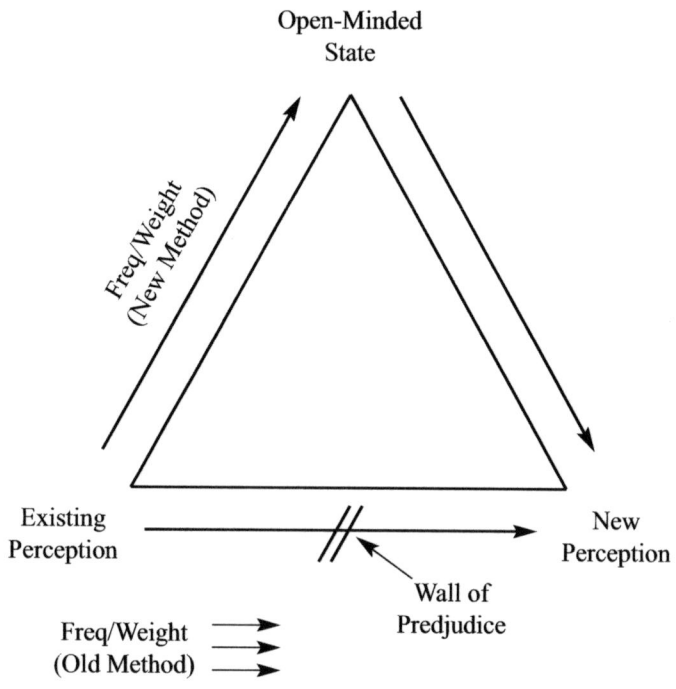

Figure 15: The open-minded state

Traditionally marketing communications has advocated frequency and weight when it comes to solving this challenge – send enough effective messages and eventually you'll break down their prejudices and they'll move to a new set of beliefs and arrive at our desired new perception point.

There are disadvantages with this strategy. For one it is expensive if you're using traditional media and spamming if you're using a 'free stamp' method such as email. That's bad enough but there's an even bigger issue in the 21st century - the short attention span world we live in. It's difficult enough to maintain enough OTS (opportunities to see) in order to break down the audiences perceptions anyway, but now their attention spans are about the same as a goldfish – so if we're trying to present a complex message then it's near impossible to keep their attention.

But what if we look to do things a different way? What if we look to convince the audience they should merely take a look at an alternative and instil in their minds that they *may* just be missing out on something? The objective of our campaign therefore becomes *'get them into an open minded state so they are more receptive to listening to what we have to say and then allow them to find their own way to a new perception via education and information providing'*.

This model follows today's zeitgeist of permission and engagement marketing and works extremely effectively for both planning and rationalising campaigns (I've used it in real life scenarios hundreds of times. It works, it's proven and it's an app that sits in the 'well used' file of my BrainBank).

Here are three examples whereby I've taken the OMS and pivoted it into place to shed light on a client's issue;

Assist in re-launching an improved version of a product that had picked up a reputation for fault

Assist in creating an internal campaign to shift the mindset of a cynical workforce

And the most important to us in terms of this book...

Changing the perception of our potential high value client from 'you're just another agency' to 'I must work with your agency'

The model is very effective and can pivot through all the above scenarios with ease. In fact, all the most successful models during the past 50 years have followed the principle of being easy to understand and adapt to your own particular circumstances – SWOT, Scorecards, the Boston Matrix, the SBU, the Long Tail, Permission Marketing, Tribalism... they are all models that can pivot to face many challenges – your most successful ones will do to.

Deductive and inductive principles

There are two basic types of logical structure when constructing apps – I categorise them as either deductive or inductive.

Deductive models
These are mathematical – for example – if we have a rule that says all sales campaigns should allow for an ROI of $X then there's no doubting where we are going. It's like the logical path we follow when someone asks us what is the answer to two plus two. We know it's four (unless you're talking to a mathematician who may wish to debate this with you).

Inductive models
These are more lateral and open to interpretation. For example, if we have a rule that says all customers should love our brand then this is open to interpretation – have you tried defining 'love' recently? It's really down to your own personal perceptions and experiences.

Being aware of this deductive / inductive distinction will assist you in choosing the right tools for the job. I've a bias towards inductive tools for creative thinking and a handful of deductive ones for investment justification (ensure the deductive 'logic' you use relates to reality however and isn't just logical in its own right. For example, all agencies are run by pink elephants, pink elephants like blue skies therefore all those who run agencies like blue skies. Logically correct, but I've not seen any elephants in an agency to date - let alone elephants that like blue skies. Sound ridiculous? I've attended presentations where the argument pedalled holds to the same structure and logic as the above). It really depends upon your agency culture, the client challenge and offering but both models are powerful in their own right.

Clients taking control

It's within the client's nature to want to take control. They run a business and they are used to taking decisions and leaving others in their wake. I promise, many of my clients are people at the top of their game and the reason we're good friends is that I tell them the truth - I tell them how it is without holding back – I take control because that's what they are paying me to do. So ensure you don't allow the client to drive the relationship - develop a robust process and take control – they will reward you handsomely for it.

Creativity – keeping it fresh

Your BrainBank should be an ever evolving organism. Consider 3M and their objective of having 33% of their profits from products 3 years of age or under. Within your BrainBank library, if a principle or tool works then keep it, discard the rest and promise to add a new one to each assignment – this way your BrainBank will continue growing and evolving and you will grow organically and never be left behind the innovation curve.

Branding your apps

The key reason we create apps is to have products that we can take to market as an entrepreneur. To this end, how we brand them is important. There are basically 3 levels to consider when branding apps - agency, your BrainBank and your apps. Here are some examples of how these three levels have been utilised;

Agency	BrainBank	APP Example
Brains on Fire	Brains on Fire	The 10 Principles
TBWA	Disruption	Brand Wheel
Ideo	Design Thinking	Innovation Venn
Kunde & Co	Corporate Religion	The Hurdle Race
Saatchi&Saatchi	Lovemarks	The Love/Respect Matrix

There is no one correct way to brand your BrainBank or apps. The key is to keep in mind the No.1 objective – produce products that will be effective in the market place and inspire clients to engage with you - which is the subject of the next section

Part 3

Lead client engagements. Never be led.

It's time to wake up to a new reality.

To take our genius to market.

To decide who we do business with.

To experience extraordinary levels of growth.

It's time to lead client engagements.

And never to be led.

It's time to wake up

Mass marketing is dying because it is being rendered ineffective. This has resulted in the mass market pitch being no longer as profitable as it was. Now, it's the long tail where the marketing opportunities lie – not in the 'pitch for everything' scenario. Clients are reinventing their businesses and their marketing departments in the wake of the new all-connected revolution. They need guides and gurus in this brave new world. Therefore, the opportunity is there to find the right model that taps into a particular market's zeitgeist and find yourself knocking on open doors. So don't pitch like an agency – pitch like an entrepreneur, codify your approach and brand it as a product. Control the process and the client by deciding who you're going to target and why (although always allow for market feedback and learn from it constantly – see roadmap at the end of this book for more details regarding suggested process).

The law of duality

Shifting the power structure away from clients and towards your agency is very appealing and you'll be tempted to approach it wholesale. But doing things with a big bang, across the whole business, is not always a sound strategy. It really depends upon the situation you find yourself in presently. The key questions to ask are;

Is your current new business activity likely to provide more than a 20% uplift this year?

Is an entrepreneurial culture in your business a large shift in style?

Are you a business with more than 50 employees?

The more you answer 'yes' to the above, the more you should launch the SuperDrive approach alongside your existing activities because you'll want to maintain that 20% + uplift, introduce an entrepreneurial culture at a measured pace and gain internal buy-in over time.

If you're running both at the same time, ensure you have your best team 100% behind SuperDrive and focus on gaining success early on. The more it is successful, the more the rest of the company will radiate towards it. And it is always more powerful if the team come to the concept rather than have it forced upon them.

Introduce it across both new business and account mgmt to work on controlled projects. Pick low hanging fruit, and then allow the principles to be adopted across the business over a period of 9 to 12 months.

A real step change in growth rates

Traditional incremental new business growth ratios normally create glass ceilings in agencies. To understand this self imposed limitation, let's assume that;

An agency normally has around 10 major clients

These accounts for around 80% of its business

The other 20% of its revenue is normally spread across a multitude of small clients / projects

The attrition rate of the business is around 25% per annum

Networking, WOM and other new business activity normally account for 3 wins of financial note per annum

Taking the above;

$100 = rev$

$80 = 10$ major clients

$0.8 =$ average valued client

0.25 = business lost per annum

0.3 = the value of networking, WOM & new business activity

You can see from the above dynamic, if the business runs with these figures year in year out it hits a glass ceiling. Chances are, the directors are good at new business and won 10 new clients during its first 2 years of existence. Since then they've been as busy maintaining those clients most of the time.

The agency has also set a norm within itself for client value, margins, new business methods, speed of change within the business and its culture. These norms result in new business that is a repeat of what's gone before. WOM brings in similar clients because they are all part of your existing network, you win 3 new clients (reality is they come in just due to the gravity pull the business has) and things stay in a comfortable stasis (assuming your margins are good and maintained) - plus or minus 10%.

Warning: You won't find extraordinary growth by looking inside your business and doing the above.

You'll need to inject something else into the business. And that's where the entrepreneurial approach excels. Remember - you take control of what you sell and who you engage with. You set the agenda. Imagine another 3 clients with an average lifetime value double your existing client base? This is the target you can set yourself via SuperDrive – if you so wish. You'd then step up from $80k to $160k per new win. Do this on top of existing activity and in 3 years you're in a different place altogether as an agency – that's SuperDrive growth.

It's a tough road. Some agencies decide to utilise it for more modest levels of growth. Some to achieve amazing levels of growth – it really is your choice. But such step change in average client value is a key factor to more dead sure profitability and growth within your agency (it may not be a higher average value client you're looking for but a shift in market emphasis, or type of work – how you utilise this step change is really down to how you wish to move your agency forward).

The push and pull debate

New business arrives either via inbound enquiries (generated via WOM, networking or the amount of social capital you have online) or outbound new business activity (telemarketing, chemistry meetings, introductory agencies, et al).

Pull always looks to be the most appealing for the following reasons;

There's no need to sell to them – after all, they came to you

They have a live brief (we assume they are not just tyre kicking)

They must have found something appealing about you in the first place (recommendation via a friend or they were impressed with your social media presence)

Pull always looks very appealing – business coming through the door – it just sounds like heaven. No wonder the blog has become the new business department's new darling. The theory goes that you can write an interesting and informative blog, potential customers will find it, read it and be so impressed with your approach they will hire you. This does work to a degree and should be pursued (your BrainBank should have enough interesting data to write an engaging blog). After all, you need to have a credible social peer index anyway because potential clients will always check you out online. But the reality is it will not be a panacea 99.99% of the time.

There are also some disadvantages to inbound enquiries such as;

The client sets the agenda and therefore maintains control

Enquiries are often not from ideal clients (wrong brief, no money, etc.) and therefore the time and energy required to win the business renders them not profitable (but we all still pitch to such clients because it's income – very few of us resist)

You may not want the business but it came via a personal recommendation so we feel obliged to run with it

You cannot predict demand very well (it's hard to predict when the phone will ring or an email ping)

So it's important to realise that inbound isn't always the panacea you may think it is. The fact is both are important. If you sit down, write and blog and wait for them to beat a path to your door then you'll be disappointed 12 months down the line when you've not had 50 major blue chips knocking on your door. But if you utilise your blog to raise your social profile and credibility then it will reinforce everything else you are doing. Once you've impressed a client via a chemistry meeting and you're moving to proposal stage, you can bet they'll check you out online. Having a blog that gives an in-depth insight into you and your way of thinking will ensure the relationship you're looking to establish will bind and engage more effectively. Therefore, a sound social media strategy will reinforce your new business activity but by itself it's not going to bring the type of business growth you'll need to see a respectable ROI. Once more for the hard of hearing;

Social media will reinforce your closing abilities but it will not reliably bring you face to face with ideal clients month in month out.

Outbound activity on the other hand means you control the when, who, why and what for of each point of contact. It is also worth considering the fact that when you win better clients via hard-earned outbound activity, your inbound enquiries also rise in quality – because the new network you're building is of a higher calibre.

So keep in mind that a healthy balance of both is essential to the success of your new business strategy. Always remember that hiding behind the comfort of inbound to the detriment of outbound will limit the growth potential of your business and not allow for exponential growth. It's your choice. Where do you want to be in 3 years?

The open minded state

Once you've accepted the concept of taking a unique product to market the whole new business dynamic changes. You are now in control. You are not giving all the power to the client by begging for a brief or being grateful for a RFP.

What happens now is down to what you decide to do. Yes, briefs will come your way (and the app is a powerful weapon in a formal pitch / RFP situation). But you can really exploit all its advantages when you decide to become pro-active and drive new business).

The key paradigm shift is that you are not looking for permission to be on a client's next pitch list. Rather, you are simply looking to inspire the client via your app and then engage with them on your own terms.

I use the 'open-minded state' model to structure any SuperDrive campaign (I outlined this model earlier – here it is in action again – demonstrating its versatility)

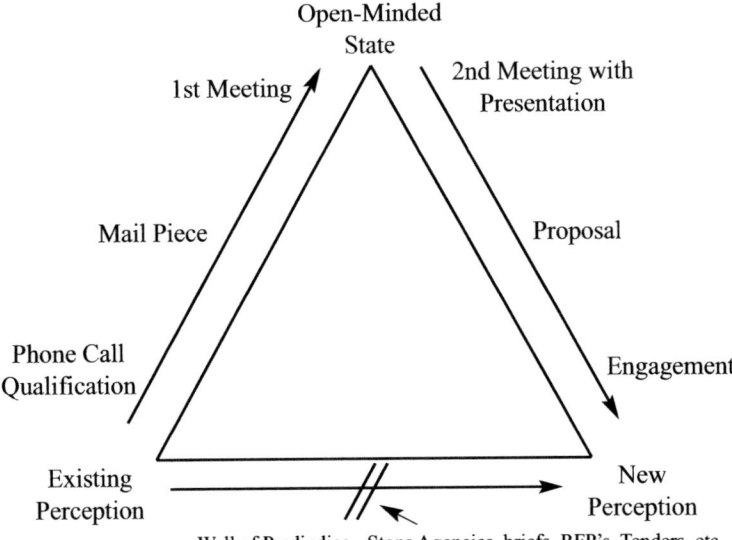

Figure 16: The open-minded state (new business campaign)

Let's say our new business objectives are very simple (and they should be). We wish to find high value new clients. We've a list of those we'd like to do business with. Should we write a blog and hope they find it? Should we email or call them and ask if they'd like to subscribe to our CRM programme in some format or other? Should we arrange chemistry meetings at which we ask if we can be included on their next brief or tender request?

The standard agency approach would undertake exactly the above activities. But then ask yourself, what would an entrepreneur do? An entrepreneur would make it his/her business to know exactly who he wanted to do business with. He would then consider the most effective way to make contact with that person (realising you've only one chance to make a first impression). It's a fine balance at this point as he would want to mitigate the possibility of the person wanting to say 'no' without a tacky, pushy sales pitch (because entrepreneurs know this would place them in a weak negotiating position).

So the entrepreneur thinks less about CRM programmes and pitches and more about ideal clients and getting his inspiring product in front of them. He knows that if he can do that, his apps will do the rest. So he decides it's his task to move the client from their existing perception (I don't need another agency) to a new perception (I really should be using this agency for competitive advantage).

But our entrepreneur realises that this potential client is constantly bombarded by agencies via email and the phone to such an extent he's built up an effective patter for ridding himself of them within 60 seconds. So no email, exclusive online invitation or telephone call is really going to be effective in getting to see this potential client.

So the entrepreneur thinks – how can I get this person to at least think, "I might be missing something here, let's take a look at this outfit." It's not going to be the reasons most agencies give; we know your sector, we wondered if you had a brief in mind, have you an RFP on the horizon. Potential clients hear this all the time. But the agency who says – "we've a unique product that is dealing with X issue – it's proven itself with A, B and C and we believe it's directly relevant to your business" - will gain the potential client's attention (assuming you're hitting the right hot buttons with your proposition – more of this later).

The above will intrigue the client who will ask for clarification. And, if what you say thereafter is credible you'll get an audience at least 20% of the time. Now just think about that hit rate – you're targeting dream clients and seeing 20% of them. If you can perform in front of said client then these will be life changing moments for the agency.

A note on setting them up for the call; I see it as a three stage process. I like to send something to the prospect that I know will both intrigue them and instil in their mind that I mean business. I still think the physical medium is the most effective (it's even more effective now because we get less post. In the UK, they don't call it the 'Royal' Mail for nothing). I've sent, books, papers I've published, bottles of whiskey with a penitent message, etc. The key is to use both logic and magic in the right dose when developing your calling card. If you sound too anal with your strategy spiel they'll just turn off. If you sound like a joker then they'll not want to do business with you. So pitch it just right. Let's just say the tone and message will be driven by the type of agency and what sort of individual you are. It is important these align because you'll need to be 110% confident when following it up.

So produce a calling card that's right on cue and follow up with the right phone call and you'll have them in a state of intrigue – they're not required to promise a brief - we're not asking for one, nor are we asking for anything at this point more than the opportunity to introduce our app and outline how we think it may be directly relevant to some of the issues they may be facing. Do your job and they'll now be in an open minded state – willing to listen. Then it's your goal to lead them through the logic of why they should now do business with you (more later on this). But for now notice the difference between this approach and the traditional agency approach:

Decide who you really want to do business with – true high LTV (lifetime value) winners.

Approach them without asking for a brief or an RFP – approach them with a new set of apps that you believe could add value to their business.

State that you're not going to bore them with case studies and a slideshow profiling your business – rather – in 10 slides you'll outline how your apps add value.

You can even explicitly state you're not looking for a brief or pitch scenario – put the prospect at ease so they don't feel they are about to be sold to.

Realise that to move the client from their existing perception (I've enough agencies on my books thank you) to the desired new perception (I should look at this agency with a view to working with them) is two meetings away – your first objective is to get them into an open minded state – new perception is further down the line.

Ensure you 'interrupt' them with an effective introductory piece – email and the telephone will come into play but they will not be effective enough in the first instance – for me – something physical is the answer. Something that's taken effort, something that says you mean business (and ensure you go through the 3 stage process – ring and ask for permission to send the piece, send it, follow it up over the phone).

Realise that your blog and online presence is a credibility enforcer – they'll check you out prior to meeting you and if what they find doesn't ring true they'll blow you out.

Remember, it's nice to sit planning white papers and online campaigns – but it will not place your new business activity in SuperDrive – don't be busy doing 'nice' tasks rather than doing the 'essential' tasks (for 'essential' read 'results' focused tasks)

The advantages of having no brief or rfp

It's often thought that the first objective a new business strategy must focus upon is 'find more briefs'. As previously outlined, this obsession has rendered agencies subservient to the client. Formal briefs, pitches and RFPs result in ensuring you play by the clients rules - often resulting in your agency becoming commoditised.

If you change the rules and make it your first objective to simply introduce them to your app portfolio, then you chose who to target and when. If you're targeting the right sort of clients (i.e. those with a propensity to be doing 'stuff' with budgets) then you don't need to ensure there is a need – you know there is as long as they believe you are the ultimate solution (the reality is clients don't see agencies for the fun of it. They genuinely are looking for new partners – it's for you to convince them they cannot live without your app without appearing hard sell and without them feeling pressured into something in the early stages. It really is the art of selling without selling – medical consultants are a classic example of this approach – they have an authority and a matter of fact approach to advice – adopt it).

The dynamics of the meeting

Let's say you've convinced a prospect to meet with you, at the meeting he becomes sufficiently impressed with you and your app so he talks about his challenges. You offer to place a couple of his issues through your app and come back with some initial thoughts and ideas without any obligation – it's all relaxed with no agenda / pressure (except the built in pressure to impress the hell out of him at the next stage).

You meet again, you present your findings and he's blown over. You propose testing one of the ideas. You suggest getting his internal team behind the concept so you arrange to meet 6 other people who will be involved in the test and interview each one of them for 45 minutes to gain the knowledge and information you require to verify the strategy is sound and that people within the organisation are behind the project.

You charge for the verification stage but it's a modest sum...

You've now been paid to 'pitch' and verify your ideas internally within the organisation without even a hint of a traditional pitch scenario.

Once the findings and recommendations have been presented (which the client team love because it is now their idea) the pressure to make the campaign happen starts to build. You can then close to a test run - which means developing creative and implementing the campaign - again without a pitch. So at this stage you're being paid to get to know the client and to prove you're the perfect partner. There's not a pitch in site. So, you do an amazing job and becoming appointed to another 4 projects within the first 12 months– effectively rendering the account yours – all this without a pitch in site (and remember this account is a dream one – so the potential value is extraordinary).

The value of the above will vary depending upon the agency you are and the type of work you do. But the principles remain the same – walk into their business on your terms, impress them, do a good job, get more work, build the relationship. Even if you are asked to pitch further down the line due to their internal procedures, you'll be in pole position as you've been asked to pitch based upon the strength of the work you've done for them to date – you're still new and fresh to them but you're also now a proven partner on the inside looking out (and you have all the client contacts mobile numbers because you've collected their business cards at each meeting).

Outbound lead generation ratios

Here are some thoughts regarding ratios for new business activity. They really are a guide but I have bet my mortgage on these on a number of occasions and always won.

Telephone Call to Appointment Ratio: 1:5

This is based on having the right proposition, right target and the right introduction method (perfection to this level takes a number of months of testing but once you're there it's like a dollar making machine you can turn on at will). I like to ensure they cannot ignore me and are quietly impressed through the mail piece. I do this by initially calling them and asking permission to send something that I believe will be of interest (they almost always automatically say they have more than enough agencies and no briefs presently). I explain I'm not looking for a brief – I just want to send them some information regarding a model I believe would be perfect for their organisation. They often ask what it is at this point – I'm pretty general about what I say but ensure that my elevator pitch is enough for them to want to know more.

I then send something via the post – something that says this is special and not run of the mill. I've sent £100 mailers before now. It's worth repeating, the key is to get the tone and message right (again – there's another book in this one but it goes without saying that if what you send is anal and bangs on about how wonderful you are in a pompous tone you're dead. You need to be supremely confident but also relaxed about how you put this across – it's a fine balance. Obviously, it also depends upon what sort of agency you are and the culture within your business – no point in sending something that bears no resemblance to your agency – although if you're looking to reposition and place pressure on people within your agency to change this can sometimes be a good thing).

Expose your proposition to the danger of the sale – 20% conversion rate from phone to first appointment – imagine doing that with just dream clients. Target 50 dream clients – 250 key contacts – 50 high calibre client meetings in year 1. Game on. Even 30% of this ratio in the early days whilst you're perfecting your apps will still ensure a profitable return on your investment.

The one meeting per week rule

You should aim to attend one new business meeting per week. I realise this will be more than you're used to doing. But I promise if you're looking for extraordinary growth rates then you're going to have to meet these figures (you'll thank me for it when your business has achieved super growth in size in 3 years time).

There are many advantages to this rule:

You're constantly listening to the market and will structure your business based upon cold hard facts from the coal face rather than by hunches and theory

If your proposition isn't right it's better to find out early on and rectify the issues – as the saying goes – it's better to fail early if you wish to find success as quickly as possible.

New business meetings will not be some grand occasion (which they are in most agencies) if you do one regularly. You'll become more relaxed and sharp due to practice.

Your knowledge of key issues will increase 10 fold in just 12 months. You'll quickly understand clients' issues and relate them to similar issues you've found elsewhere – therefore getting on their wavelength will be instantaneous because you'll be in the zeitgeist.

Your network of important contacts will grow apace – again leading to a greater knowledge and more valuable perspective that clients will appreciate as best practice.

You'll quickly find out which apps / processes /principles work in the market place and discard the others. Those that prove themselves will become more robust and proven as time goes on

How many should you pitch to?

Let's assume you've targeted your dream target list - these are companies with high growth potential and the right cultural fit. Given this, you should often find yourself being in the last 15 minutes of the first meeting thinking 'I can help this company'. Yes, they'll be some where you'll feel the chemistry just isn't right and you'll wait to see what they commit to rather than offer anything up. However, if the chemistry fit is right then you really should be closing 50% of those you see to a second meeting at which you'll present some initial ideas. You can do less / more than this ratio but I've found this is about right.

A major caveat – if you find yourself in meetings thinking you don't want to develop any ideas as the relationship will probably go nowhere then you've probably targeted the wrong type of organisation. In my experience, if you have a killer solution to an issue then the prospect will 'like' you so the chemistry will be there almost immediately and if they are potentially a high value company then you shouldn't fear the time and investment that will be needed to gain this client's trust.

The golden numbers

Your activity levels will differ depending upon objectives. However, these numbers relate to the growth levels discussed earlier.

1 Meeting per week
48 Per Annum
24 Proposals
8 New Clients
3 New Clients become major high value clients within 12 months
5 New Clients contribute a smaller ROI but go no further (politics, fit, etc.)

Keeping all the balls in the air

I genuinely believe you'll have problems if you stick to the old pitch system in the future – the value of them will continue to fall and not warrant commoditised shoot-outs. But you'll also have problems if you leave behind those methods instantly. You're just going to have to do both for a period – yes – it's hard work but in three years you'll thank me for it.

We've already talked about the law of duality. But there is also another 'duality' principle to follow whereby we keep in mind a short and the medium term perspective (I don't like the notion of the long term because, as I used to be told by a consultant colleague, in the long term we're all dead!).

It's important that we create both short and medium term goals. Often in new business the medium term is used as a way of taking the pressure off in the short term. We've all heard the 'we've a full pipeline' or 'I'm heavily pregnant with potential business.' The reality is, if you're not meeting your short term goals then your medium terms goals will probably be not be met either. So have both.

Short term goals should include;

Number of meetings during the next quarter (aim to have at least 6 meetings booked ahead)

Number of meetings held last quarter (aim to have attended 12 – net cancellations)

Number of 2nd meeting 'proposals' attended and awaiting commitment (aim to have 4 to 7 ongoing)

Note: As a rule of thumb, you should have 7 potential pieces of business in the pipeline at any given time (this is from all sources). Any less and things can start to look thin quickly if you have a quick succession drop away. It will take you 6 to 12 months to get to the above average numbers but once you're there don't let the figures fall off as this will choke off your new business pipeline.

So keep up your WOM, CRM, AAR, RFP and Social Media programmes. These will never go away – and you'll pick up formal briefs, pitches and RFPs whilst undertaking your app programme. The aim is to enhance your new business programme with a process that will take you to the next level of growth – a programme that will take you to exponential levels of growth. As I've said, this method will not work instantly. It normally takes 12 months to get the process honed and all the personnel within the business 100% behind it. By year 2 it really will start to pick up and become a tool that generates as many dream clients as you want (see back of book for timetable details).

Expose yourself to the danger of the sale

You've developed some apps. Now is the time to take them to the market. Until you expose them to the danger of the sale they remain unproven. Once they are in the market you'll know what works and what doesn't very quickly. You'll also be able hone the promising apps into killer sales tools very quickly – as I've already said, there's nothing like a live client to expose the weak or ill thought through idea.

Start immediately. Keep refining. Don't expect perfection. Don't expect everything to work from day one. But I can promise you if you maintain a relentless campaign to market, within 12 months you'll have a robust, proven set of principles that will ensure you leave the commodity market behind. I have used this model and walked into one of the largest commercial financial institutions in the world, met a middle manager, discussed his issues, arranged a second meeting at which I presented some initial thoughts and then found myself sat in front of the global VC of marketing taking a direct brief with no pitch attached within 1 month – find me a CRM or blog programme that can do the same month in month out.

Aligning your apps with key markets

Most agencies focus on particular industry sectors when looking at targeting strategy. The notion seems to be a sound one – find an industry you have experience in then seek out companies within it. There are issues with this approach. Firstly, conflict of interest always rears its head. If your experience is current (you're working with someone within that market) then potential clients will brush you away due to any potential conflict issues. If, on the other hand, your experience is based upon a past client, your experience may be dated and, more of an issue, the potential client will ask why you lost the original account in the first place. It's just not a good starting place.

Let's say you manoeuvre around the above issues (maybe you employ someone with relevant industry experience or partner with a consultant who knows the market), you enter said market and find a client. You're then in a cul-de-sac – because said new client will not let you work elsewhere within that industry – you've therefore spent considerable amounts of time building 'experience' and then taking it to a market that then has limited return potential for you due to conflict of interests. There is a better way.

Start by deconstructing your favourite app. What is it that renders it so effective? Let's say my favourite app is the 'open-minded state' model. I believe this model is powerful because it works with any campaign that is looking to change a target audience's perceptions. The model realises that you need to gain someone's attention in such a way that they are willing to listen to you, not under duress, before you can start to close them to a new way of looking at things.

Eureka! This model can be utilised in any market where fixed perceptions and prejudices hinder the launching of a new company, idea or product. And how many markets are there for such a model? You could utilise it for internal stakeholder markets, product launches, re-launches, repositioning, direct sales, corporate sales, et al. The list is endless.

At this point you have the luxury of picking the most appealing companies for various disciplines, scenarios or from any relevant vertical. You don't need to just to make up the database numbers to justify the effort placed into creating a vertical campaign. You can invest effort in your app and see almost a limitless return because the potential market is so huge – you'll never need to compromise with regards to who you target again.

So the golden rule is – deconstruct your favourite app so you understand what makes it effective and then find others that require that dynamic. This approach will arm you with unique propositions that can work through many markets.

Another advantage to segmentation by app need is that it decreases your reliance on particular verticals. For example, if you major in high street retail or b2b construction, all you need is a sector downturn and your business falls off a cliff. If on the other hand you have a killer app that works across a handful of diverse sectors, any market downturn can be offset against others that are booming.

You'll also never have to sit in a meeting claiming you know a client's market better than they do. I just hate this – if you do know the market better than they do they often see you as a threat and if you don't (which is normally the case if you're dealing with senior management) then you quickly lose credibility (as a rule of thumb – get to know the basic dynamics of a market quickly using the cascading rule of three app outlined previously – that will give you a sufficient depth of knowledge in an hour's focused desk research).

A word about middle mgmt and decision makers

You hear it said that you need to see top management in order to make things happen. This can be true. But often I've found ambitious middle managers are brilliant catalysts and they are often the people who 'do' things within an organisation. The marketing director may often be so far removed from the cliff face that they genuinely have nothing on the horizon. Also, it can be a disadvantage to go top down (from marketing director's blessing to middle management) as you may find middle management resent having you foisted upon them. Ultimately there is no right or wrong and you won't understand the dynamic within an organisation until you enter it. Just keep in mind top down isn't always the answer.

Keep in the forefront of your mind it's targeting the right potential clients to start with that really matters – get this wrong and nothing else will rectify it. When you're compiling a list of ideal clients, don't see it as a chore that you should get out of the way in a couple of hours because you want to get the programme up and running. Your target list should grow organically – some from a data house, others from market reports, others you see in the press, some that you have a tip off about

– they are all relevant as long as you have a set of key selection criteria and you stick to them within reason (there are always one or two that you will target for other reasons – the Creative Director wants it for example).

Criteria for targeting may include some of the following;

They would be a high value client (they have a big budget and spend it on the things we do)

They have a propensity to innovate (they do stuff)

They are marketing driven (let's preach to the converted)

Their culture would 'fit' with ours (if we're a creative hot house then no funeral directors please)

They would add to our portfolio strategically (we could enter a highly valuable market via this client)

You could easily set up a scorecard system –and score each of the above out of 20. Anything that scores less than 70 doesn't go on the list (I scan-read data and do this in my head these days but if you've a committee making the targeting decisions then a more formal approach may help).

Try to be positive when scoring them. If you've been in the business for some years it's easy to say, 'I've been to this company before and it's a waste of time'. If they have a large budget and fit other criteria then you really should consider them. Sometimes a new approach makes things happen.

Targeting logic

Targeting strategy is not just about choosing sectors and picking data.

As we've seen, you should also be looking at potential needs across verticals as it opens up many more avenues of opportunity. And there are many other ways of finding rich streams of new business opportunity. Here are some examples I've utilised in the past successfully;

Ambitious middle management

Under 35s high flyers (they'll give you 20 years of value – market trade journals have a list of them every year!)

Top 100 fastest growing companies (by sector is a popular one)

Innovative companies (they may be financing themselves via AIM or NASDAQ or some other means which tells you they are dynamic and forward thinking)

Power 100 lists in the trade press journals

The campaign structure

Brain Bank > App Dev > Targeting > Qualification >

Interruption > Chemistry Meeting > Intrigue Creation > Brief > Presentation Development

Presentation Meeting > Proposal > Verification > Test > Roll-Out

Figure 17: The new business value chain

BRIANBANK
Our formal depository centre where raw data is made available, analysed and articulated into a usable format

APP DEVELOPMENT
Data from BrainBank is combined to produce processes and principles (all directed by our approach and outlook as a company)

TARGETING
Based upon uses found for apps (it may be that targeting comes before app development if you have a particular market to target)

QUALIFICATION
Outbound qualification process via online or telephone enquiries

INTERRUPTION
Thought piece that sparks their imagination and interest and gains credibility

OMS
Point of contact requesting chemistry meeting – aim to get potential client into an OMS so they are prepared to learn more about your app – not to ask for a brief and RFP at this stage

CHEMISTRY MEETING
1:1 meeting utilising the 3i's – inspire, interrogate and ignite – objective – to gain insight into client's key issues and agree to develop some initial thoughts based around them (with no obligation to the client except a second meeting)

INTRIGUE
The state of mind of the potential client should be post meeting (they are looking forward to seeing what your thoughts are re: their issues)

BRIEF
The approach, processes and principles (apps) used to frame the brief

PRESENTATION DEVELOPMENT
The approach, processes and principles (apps) used to frame presentation development

PRESENTATION MEETING
Format based upon app – honed and designed to inspire

PROPOSAL
Format based upon app and designed to reassure and ignite (i.e. 3D approach – discover, devise and deliver)

VERIFICATION
Internal and external research using app tool to verify logic of proposal (designed to reassure and ignite complete DMU within the client's organisation)

TEST
Pilot activity if possible / required in order to reassure

ROLL OUT
Both above campaign and other campaigns within organisation as relationship matures

NB. A formal pitch or RFP may rear its head during this value chain so be prepared to improvise and utilise the app to derail and add value to the process. You may also find that upon presenting your ideas, the contact suggests another project with a tighter deadline, etc. The key is to remain flexible whilst still politely driving through and maintaining control of the process.

Using the app to drive RFPs and traditional pitch new business

The app is also a major tool when it comes to driving traditional new business processes such as the pitch and RFP. As we outlined above, the entrepreneurial approach demands that you take control of the who, what, how and when of new business activity and that the key is having the right mechanism for breaking the ice with your chosen partners – after all, you've chosen to make contact with them and this time you're not going to start down the road of meekly asking if they have a brief or up and coming pitches they can control you by. Instead, you're contacting them as one business to another with a business proposition. A proposition that states – you have a unique app that can add value to their business and you'd like to outline your thoughts face-to-face. But what about in the face of traditional new business scenarios you may ask?

Again, the agency app can be an extremely flexible tool. Here are some common examples;

Formal RFPs
If you simply jump through the hoops they provide you with how would you expect to differentiate yourself? Utilise the app to suggest a different approach. Maybe still fill in their forms and provide the app driven proposal as a differentiator.

Formal Pitches

Pitches from cold are always a challenge for the following reasons; difficulty of gaining an inside track, lack of informal brainstorming with client, difficulty getting to the truth regarding internal agendas, a very short amount of time within which you can attempt to build a relationship and get to understand the client. In such circumstances, apps are a powerful way of taking some control back from the client. Here are some examples of how the app can be used in a formal pitch situation;

If your app has a verification or test process built into it allow the client to commit simply to this rather than to the whole project (you are now a commercially logical choice because your recommendations can be tested quickly and cost effectively)

If your app requires client insight on a 1:1 basis, request that this is done prior to the pitch in order to gain as much insight into the company as possible (5 or 10 internal interviews will reveal many facets to the business)

Create audience participation during the formal presentation utilising appropriate app tools in order that the client gains insight and buy-in to your thinking and conclusions

If you're being asked to re-pitch your agency, a new app can assist in revitalising the relationship and bring a new dynamic to the account

Asking if they have a brief over the phone

There's a simple rule when making calls looking for business – don't immediately ask them if they have a brief or a budget. If you've done your homework then they'll have briefs and budgets (you've targeted high value clients so they'll do stuff all the time). If they divulge the fact they have an up and coming pitch scenario then its fine to discuss it and drill down as far as they'll allow you to. Remember – your key objective is to place them in a state of intrigue (our OMS) so they agree to an exploratory meeting. Asking for more just makes you sound pushy and unprofessional. The key is to have a very compelling elevator pitch which leaves them wanting more.

Preparing for meetings

I've met new business professionals that proudly tell me they've prepared for days before a new business meeting. At that precise moment I think they are either very new to the game, they are targeting the wrong market or they are going to bore the recipient with facts they probably already know. If they then ask me which case studies they should take I give up (clients are not interested in them – they are interested in themselves – case studies are leave behinds or asides – they are not the key to a successful chemistry meeting).

Rather, if you've targeted someone based on the fact you have an app / method that will work within their business then you should only need an hour or two of desk research (including booking your flight, sorting your directions out and getting your slides together). Remember, you know your methodology inside out. When you decided to target a particular company you were certain the models would apply to their business. All you need to do now is have one slide outlining some of the possible areas of their business you are interested in.

Your whole presentation should have approximately 6 to 12 slides maximum. As an example;

Pre-amble whilst getting things set up – This is the time to provide company detail and case studies in hard copy as leave behinds

Slide 1 – Why we are here? To introduce app (reality is you're there to inspire them to open up and talk through their issues but it sounds a little pushy this early in the presentation. If they are impressed they'll open up naturally).

Slide 2 - Issues Marketers are facing

Slide 3 – How the app can be applied to these issues

Slide 4 – app model outlined

Slide 5 – Allude to success elsewhere (no case study detail just name of organisations and outcomes)

Slide 6 – How we thought the app might apply to said business (caveat this by stating you realise you're second guessing their issues and you're more interested in their take on the situation)

Slide 7 – A slide that says – over to the client as you're fascinated to understand more about the dynamics of their business

Then wait for the response. Normally they will start to pre-amble with their corporate background script. Start to probe with questions in order to encourage them to open up. If they have been impressed with you up to this point they will open up (especially if you've casually advised them you're not on a mission for a formal brief and that you're not going to hard sell them).

Other background research

Some thoughts regarding pre-meeting research - look at their SBUs (strategic business units) and consider how they break down. Consider what remit the person you're meeting may have in this dynamic. Look at the last chairperson's statement and consider the areas of most interest to the business (use a little NLP by using the phrases and concepts the chairperson is using during conversation). Look at the key issues in their market by taking a look at the headlines online in their three major trade blogs / journals. Consider how your models may possibly apply – think about these in the shower / whilst driving / etc. Which areas of the marketing mix are going to be interesting to them – product, positioning, differentiation, sales to key markets, key account mgmt, seminars, events, online presence, offline presence, ability to move quickly – take a look at the wheel of products in this book – the client really could take it anywhere during the meeting so think through scenarios in your mind).

The key is – assume nothing. Have all this in your head. Your mission is to knock them dead in 15 minutes with your methodology and relate it to their business in generic teams (caveat your assumptions very early on and ask for clarification – they will appreciate this and it will encourage them to open up).

Gaining credibility in the first 15 minutes

The first 15 minutes are about you gaining credibility. Get this right and the rest of the meeting will be about them. So how do you gain credibility within that amount of time? First of all I'm assuming you've done everything right up to this point – sent them something which impressed them to such an extent they'd listen to you on the phone and post phone call they were intrigued enough to want to meet you and they found your online presence impressive. If any of the above fall you'll be off to a bad start.

The corridor chat is always more important than you think. On the way in it's about deciding whether you initially both like each other. You'll find as a matter of course most conversations will include the classic get out clause – 'I've only 45 minutes' and 'I'm not sure why we scheduled this meeting in the first place'. Both these statements are put offs for agencies doing the hard sell and immediately seeking pitches and briefs. Normally it's just a smoke screen. We're all grown up and no one forces us into professional meetings – they've taken the time to schedule this meeting and they've probably checked you out online prior to the meeting so they obviously think a meeting is possibly relevant – they just don't want to commit early on and then have to retreat awkwardly if you're not what they hoped for.

I always start the meeting by explaining we have a unique model which I believe is possibly (notice how relaxed 'possibly' sounds) relevant to their business and I'd simply like their opinion. I state I'm not looking for a brief or a chance to look at an RFP (unless they seem to have a burning desire for me to do so). This reassures the client and takes the meeting to a more relaxed place.

I then, in less than 12 slides, set the scene (the challenges faced by marketers) and how the model can solve them (I give them a physical brochure which provides the hygiene factor stuff right at the beginning so I don't spent too much time on the obvious). I then close off the introduction by asking them to tell me more about their business and the challenges / opportunities it faces.

Present like Steve Jobs

In his book, The Perfect Pitch, Jon Steel outlines how he was invited to meet Steve Jobs to take a brief. It was 1997 and Jobs had just returned to Apple to save the company. Steve was late for the meeting so two marketers from Apple presented 1.5hrs of bar charts, background data and product information whilst they waited for Steve.

Jon was almost asleep when Steve Jobs walked into the room. But then the atmosphere changed and the room was charged with energy as Jobs outlined in 5 minutes with a marker pen and a wipe board exactly what he had planned at Apple. He took another 60 seconds to explain what he wanted from his agency.

Jon Steel places this as one of the most stimulating presentations he's ever attended (and he's been to a few I expect).

So the message is clear – don't be anal about your app. Inspire by being succinct and have conviction in what you're presenting by being yourself (Jobs was never one for corporate graces). If you try to tie everything up in charts, data and phrases that make no sense or try to make simple concepts complex, people will just switch off. So the message is clear - make a good 'Job' if it.

The new chemistry meeting dynamic

So we've established that to take a brief or be placed on a pitch doesn't need to be the no.1 agenda on your list when it comes to taking a credentials or so called chemistry meeting with a client and that often such a meeting can be a disadvantage as the potential clients starts to see you as a commodity. The new objective is to present your relevant killer app or model to said client and gain credibility and a rapport within the first 15 minutes so that they'll open up and start to discuss their business and the issues they face.

I structure the chemistry meeting in three distinct stages - the 3i's;

Inspire - This happens within the first 15 minutes – you need to set the scene and convince him via logic and magic that you have a methodology that really solves the sorts of issues he has. This is the time to utilise your handful of slides as outlined earlier.

Interrogate - The main part of the meeting (at least 45 minutes and normally 1.5 hrs if things are going well). At this stage its 80:20 in his favour regarding who does the talking. Lead with questions. Again, we've not the space to cover this subject in depth but remember to demonstrate understanding and empathy by asking interesting questions. If you come across as someone who's just trying to lead the client to a sales opportunity they will clam up and become defensive. Keep it open and be genuinely interested in their business (I always try to imagine I'm about to purchase their business and really want to know what I'm buying and what it would be worth to me. That really helps keep me on track and focused).

Ignite – The last 10 minutes of a meeting. This is the time when you should have a good idea of the issues you could help them with. You need to be firm but relaxed at this point and advise the client you're going to look at 'X' particular issue as discussed. Reassure them you're not looking for commitment at this point. If they feel you're closing them to anything more than another meeting they'll become defensive. Listen to which of the highlighted issues they seem the most interested in (sometimes this will have been clear during the meeting but sometimes it's not forthcoming because the client is afraid of making any commitment).

Step by logical step

They definitely run in this order – if you cannot inspire then you'll not be able to interrogate because the said potential client will just not open up. He'll provide you with 45 minutes of facts about the business and then politely round off by promising to be in touch when some sort of pitch comes up (they normally promise something in around 3 to 6 months – this really is a sign that they don't think you can help them in nearly all cases).

If you don't interrogate them properly then you'll not be able to get under the skin of their issues and identify the areas where your model could be applied.

Assuming you get through the first two stages, you then have to consider which of the issues you'd like to place through your app (I always like to ring 2 or 3 issues and then say I'd like to help with all of them and wait to see which the client lands on). At this point you need to ignite the relationship by firmly stating you're going to look at said issue but do this in a relaxed manner (strong, professional and relaxed – think consultant in a hospital for tone of voice at this stage) and clearly state that you are not looking for a commitment at this stage at all – just his counsel.

Which issue?

Whilst in the chemistry meeting, consider some of the following dynamics in order to make the right decisions;

Is this person someone who's opinion will be respected within this business?

Could they 'sell' me within this business?

Are the issues chosen important to them?

Does it sound like something that will happen in the next 6 months?

What is the personal chemistry like?

Remember, that it's easier to talk yourself out of business than the converse. Be positive. Remember, you're looking to win their heart – the project you present might not take its initial form by the time it comes to life – it's sole reason for being is to engage with the client so you can start to build the relationship and get on their roster list. If they insist on you joining a formal pitch process – try to engage them via your app process in order to differentiate yourself and derail the competition.

Getting the information you want by asking for it during a first meeting

There is only one way to find out about a clients business – listen to what they have to say and ask the right questions to keep the conversation moving along. They normally start with a big overview – you should have an idea of the big picture based upon your pre meeting desk research. Choice questions that demonstrate you are engaging with and understanding the client are essential at this point. You are looking to establish credibility so the client can think to themselves, "here is someone who speaks my language therefore I will enjoy engaging in conversation with them". They start to relax and tell you where they fit into the organisation, the challenges they face and where the business is going. All the time you keep asking the right questions, interjecting only when necessary to keep a healthy pace and focus.

Don't leap on possible opportunities, asking for a brief, unless they are directly brought up as a project by the client. Simply listen to their business objectives – showing empathy through understanding and occasionally outlining how you solved such issues in the past (each of these interjections should be no more than 15 seconds so the client can regain control of the conversation and therefore keep providing you with information).

As you explore his issues write them down with intent – it shows a high level of interest and respect. You'll normally find you'll cover a handful of areas. Highlight those which look like potential areas for opportunity.

Such a meeting may last 1.5 / 2.0 hrs. This is a good sign. When it feels like all general bases have been touched interject and ring the areas to highlight those of interest to you. Explain that they would offer the perfect opportunity to demonstrate what your apps / models / system could do for their business.

Closing the second meeting

Assuming you have avoided the traditional pitch or RFP route. Here's how to move the client forward beyond the initial chemistry meeting.

You're now at the end of the first meeting – the chemistry is there, you've discussed the client's issues and you've identified those you believe you can help with. This is now the magic moment – he'll most definitely attempt to stop you at this point and suggest he gets in touch (sometimes it moves more quickly and he wants you to take a brief / look at a particular issue, etc – if he does go with this route as he's plainly engaged).

If you leave him to get in touch, no matter how much he's been impressed with you, there is a strong possibility it will never happen. It's not that he wasn't impressed or that he doesn't intend to – it's just that things take over, he gets busy and he reverts back to the path of least resistance when he needs something doing – his existing agencies.

Rather, at this crucial moment you must take control and state you are going to look at issue X and Y. You explain you have a team whose only reason for being in to solve issues via your app methodology and you believe you can bring something back of value. Again, emphasise that at this point it is positively without any strings – stay relaxed and calm (some people feel awkward taking control and tacitly ask for permission – remember – you will always achieve much more in life by not asking for permission but by moving ahead – they are paying you to take control because you're the professional advisor). Close them for another date and ensure it's within 21 days if you possibly can (not always possible but it's best to move quickly as it will impress and the mood music within their organisation will not have changed). If he doesn't have access to his diary then suggest a date and let them know you'll send through the meeting details.

Corridor talk

This is the most relaxed part of the meeting, where you really do gain insight into how the client is feeling. I always casually ask what they are walking into post our meeting. It's amazing how much information regarding his position in the company and the dynamics that play come back in his answer.

The killer pitch structure

Once you're through round 1 it's time to develop a killer presentation that addresses the issues discussed. The key is to have a methodology to follow – this way you'll never waste time debating what's to be done. There are two drivers of a successful presentation – the strategic and the creative. Both should follow your methodology and the output should fit into a 'knock them dead' report template that utilises your apps.

Here's an example of a presentation I created which was broken down with 4 headings with a number of apps included:

Absorption: the mood music (quote back what client said), roadmap (where the client is heading – tie in with corporate overview and client's micro issues / objectives as discussed in the chemistry meeting).

Conventions: retro: competitor activity and clichés

Disruption: retro: other market models that could work in this scenario, campaign to utilise open-minded state, communications plan based around this model.

Explosion: Plan the way ahead - 3D approach – Discover (verify thoughts and ideas via research), Devise (redraw and revise concept and planning), Deliver (expose the concept to the danger of possible success / test and revise / roll out).

I could write this report in 5 hours because I spent 10 years perfecting the logic in it. The client is not paying for my 5 hours. He's paying for the 10 years I spent perfecting it. The 5 hours would be sat behind the desk researching and writing it (bullet format) and finding ways of briefing the creative team to keep them on track (or to post rationalise a lateral moment of genius they had). I would spend time in the shower, car or whenever I was doing something mundane, going through the presentation in my mind tweaking it to perfection.

When it comes to presenting the report – have hard copies as well as the use of tablets (i-pads for members of the audience really do work a treat as long as you're controlling it all centrally).

Have a report template continuation sheet produced that really looks the business (watermark your proprietary system logo in it and buy the best paper you can find). Have a front / back cover and binding system that oozes quality. They'll be impressed (the number of clients who've commented upon such attention to detail convinces me all this really does matter. In fact, I once pitched to British Airways using said format – their marketing director at the time commented out loud that they should use the same format for their tender documents. We went on to utilise many of our own apps within BA and they were a stimulating and profitable client).

The creative output will vary slightly but try to keep to a format as much as possible. I've always found a strong concept / visual adapted over various relevant media impresses the client. Use a combination of the obvious and not so obvious and try to utilise something near the present innovation curve – mobile is the choice of the day when it comes to front of the tech envelop as I write this but it changes almost quarterly these days (what you present will obviously vary immensely depending upon what service you're offering so adapt this example as required). The amount of time you spend developing your creative output is really a commercial decision. Some people recommend just developing mood boards (or IA/UX, Wireframes, etc) and a strategic document. I've found good creative teams can create campaign visuals in the same amount of time. It's really down to where your skill base lies and how efficient your team is.

As the creative team will tell you – one great idea should work effortlessly across all media (never has this been more important). You should also be able to have middleweight creative/programmers adapt the concept over various media with senior mgmt simply overseeing it. This has the advantage of exposing more junior staff to real pitch activity without allowing them to spend days bringing back irrelevant, naive ideas that have no commercial merit (we've all seen them).

One last point regarding creative output - try to bring a sense of humour to the party. We once took a delegate of clients to a mountain resort for a chemistry meeting – for fun we made up a branded breakfast pack and arranged to have them placed in each client's room – it consisted of a of a branded breakfast experience including a box of All Bran cereal with a wrap around on it stating – "here's hoping you're a regular client in 2012!" All delegates had a smile upon their face - winners all 'round! It really is the small things that relax the situation that make all the difference – utilise them.

Closing Business

Let's assume you've a winning report template and you're creative is second to none. You've presented your work and he's really impressed. At this point he'll be thinking – if they can do this off the back of a 1.5 hr conversation, what could they do for me if we had a formal relationship? He'll also have other issues going around in his mind; what if this doesn't work? Am I willing to stick my neck out? What is this going to cost? Should I give them a standard project to work on first?

Let's assume he really is convinced he wants to work with you. Give him two options – to further develop the concept you've brought back or to work on some other project (I always assume he's going ahead with the project presented unless he contradicts that. If he does – ensure he doesn't feel awkward about getting you to work at yet another project – as long as you're getting commitment from him this time it's mission accomplished).

Once it's decided what you'll work on, outline the process to him (again brand it). Here's an example of what I utilise. I call it;

3D

Discover – Suggest you need to further discuss the concept with key decision makers within his company - those that would have a hand in making the campaign a success. Agree the campaign value chain with him and then list the key DMU (decision making unit) along it. Explain that you wish to do this in order to gain further insight from his DMU and to also gain buy-in from the DMU – you need them onboard because they'll be key to ensuring the campaign is a success.

Devise – Based on the above, the original concepts would be either further developed or a new concept developed depending upon the findings.

Deliver – The media plan and timing.

The key is to allow them to commit to each stage as they wish. So let's say 'discover' costs $X and will include interviews, a workshop and a report – all following your methodology of course. You are now being paid to build relationships within the organisation itself. It will also be extremely difficult for your main contact to back out once you've undertaken these interviews because all his colleagues are now looking forward to seeing the campaign launched (they will all see the campaign as their idea).

NB. A lesson learnt early in my career when I pitched a concept and a delivery plan to a major corporation - The marketing director, a bear of a man who people genuinely were frightened of (but who became a good client and friend) told me to place all my work in a filing cabinet in his office. I did so wondering what was coming next.

He then told me to run two workshops with his sales managers and then promise them I would go away and develop some ideas based on their insight. He then told me to present what I'd presented to him in the first place using their ideas to rationalise it! It was now their idea – not managements! The campaign went on to win major awards and, more importantly, because the whole team was behind it, generated $millions in ROI. Lesson learnt! I also picked up dozens of projects (and eventually the whole account) from those I interviewed as they all ran business units of their own. Game on!

All or nothing is dying

When it comes to closing businesses, the big pitch scenario allows for a big win – or nothing. Here's a familiar tale... "So the whole campaign looks like being at least a $Million in fee plus media. We need commitment Mr Client. We cannot do anything for you for less" agencies say. That worked in the old mass marketing world (and there are still some of these brands left and SuperDrive is perfect for them – long may they continue). However, more often now clients want to test, innovate and prove concepts before making big commitments (but remember, if the client still insists on an all or nothing pitch then get your apps ready – they are a major weapon in the agency commodity war).

It's now a fact that the large formal pitch structure is becoming less effective as a money generating machine for agencies. All that effort, very little return and treated like a commodity throughout the whole process – life's a pitch as they say. Yes, we'll always do them – but we must remember our apps allow us to go beyond the subservient land of RFPs and into a place where we take control.

We own our unique proprietary system. We chose to target the client, we chose which areas of his business we believe we can help him with. Now all we need to do is take control. We can now go ahead and choose our own destiny.

How to make your agency 'happy'

The clichéd route to happiness is a place called nirvana. A place where there's no pressure, life is perfect and all challenges are met. However, a number of psychologists have a very different take on what makes us happy. They have found that those that experienced the following had the highest level of happiness in their lives;

Intensely focused on an activity that is of their own choosing

They were neither under-challenged (boreout) nor over-challenged (burnout)

They had a clear objective

They received immediate feedback

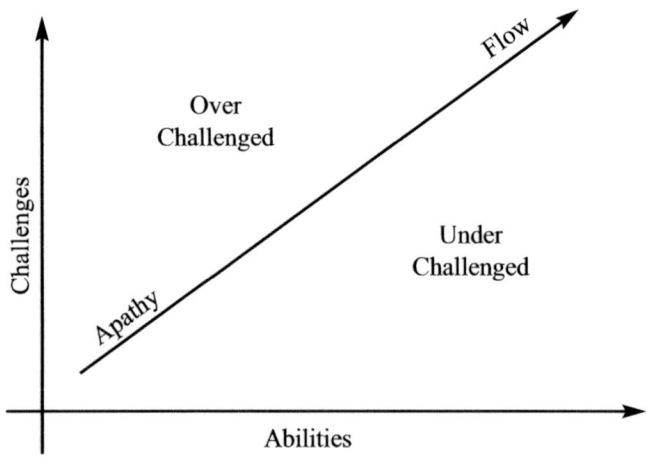

Figure 18: The happiness model

Those experiencing the above entered a life that 'flowed' naturally. To me it's almost like the 'zone' musicians and sports people talk of experiencing. Now imagine what such happiness could bring if everyone within your agency experienced it as they entered the building every morning. By building a unique methodology, by getting all the team involved in developing it and using it daily you'll do just that;

They'll be focused

They'll be challenged (but not over challenged)

They will have clear objectives – for new business, for account management, for creating new ideas, for knowing how things are to be done

They will receive immediate feedback because clients will tell them what works and what doesn't

Existing account mgmt

Your app brand can also be used with existing clients (and really should be). It can help;

Revitalise existing accounts

Focus your account mgmt team

Assist in cross-sell and up-sell (new models that clients didn't know about)

Often too much emphasis is placed upon producing brilliant ideas to win new clients. Your apps can restore the balance by producing focused, powerful ideas for your existing accounts.

Scaling up or down

All the examples in this chapter – scale them up or down depending upon the size of your business. The key principle is to ensure you adapt your processes to the long tail... if you don't then you'll start to lose ground to the competition.

If you're in a large corporation then the entrepreneurial approach maybe alien presently. But you have the advantage of brilliant minds in abundance. Your BrainBank and consequent apps will have a larger intellectual resource to draw from and the entrepreneurial nature of the SuperDrive approach will improve moral and initiative.

If you're a small, boutique agency, then you'll be used to an entrepreneurial approach and will realise that the long tail phenomenon is like being in a sweet shop presently – with opportunities simply everywhere you look. The secret in this case is to remain focused upon high value-added accounts (it may be that you're the 3rd agency on the roster but if the client has overall a £10m budget this is just fine).

Timescales

Developing an entrepreneurial approach is not difficult in theory. In practice however it's really down to the type of culture and skill set you presently have within your business. If the culture is one of being reactive to RFPs, briefs and pitches and not one of proactively advising clients and taking control of the relationship, it will be alien in the early days.

I can assure you however that the feeling of liberation when you finally have taken control of the new business process and clients are following your instructions will make all the pain worth it!

I have worked with companies that have the intellectual and social tools required from day 1 and therefore they see returns almost immediately. I have also worked with organisations who have found the concept of proactively 'selling' a proprietary product alien and it's taken as long as two years before they finally 'got it' to such a degree they were able to decide who they wanted to work with and close them without an issue.

The average app integration should look at 12 weeks for developing a set of tools and then a year to sell a handful of projects whilst refining and honing them. During that first 52 weeks the reality is you'll never know whether or not a particular proposition will be successful. It will not be until you've 'exposed it to the danger of the sale' that you'll know if it's working 100% or not. There's nothing like a real life potential client sat opposite your neat and tidy presentation to find out what works and what doesn't.

You need to keep refining, adding, subtracting and perfecting your model(s). This is the key to success. As you refine them and learn how clients react you'll become deeply knowledgeable and be able to anticipate the clients every thought. The process through to sale will become natural. You'll be in control and the client will thank you for it. After all, that's what they are paying you for!

By year 2 you'll have a methodology that both existing and new clients' value. You'll be able to set goals and decide upon who you wish to work with and then go and work with them – building a relationship in a healthy, natural way – via stimulation and trust built over a natural period of time. And certainly not like the artificial pitch scenario that could be likened to a rebound wedding - the client has decided to get divorced having fallen out of love with their existing agency. They've meet 5 agencies and spent less than 5 hours with each – suspecting each will say anything to win the work because they are motivated by money as much as anything else. They then decide which one they possibly could stay married too, based upon this artificial scenario. No wonder most end in divorce!

A sound relationship is nearly always built naturally over a long period of time. Each party tests each other's integrity. Small things during the early days matter. But each positive outcome reinforces each parties desire to maintain the relationship until one day they are close partners. This is not what happens in the typical brief / pitch scenario. This is what will happen if you follow the SuperDrive methodology to new business.

Part 4

The way ahead

SuperDrive is a way of working, a method and a set of models and principles.

SuperDrive codifies your culture and your way of working.

It makes your company super effective.

It allows more time for creativity.

It allows for deep expertise to be constructed quickly.

It allows you to exploit the knowledge economy and to act less like an agency and more like an entrepreneurial hub.

So choose your destiny.

And drive there.

The SuperDrive Road Map

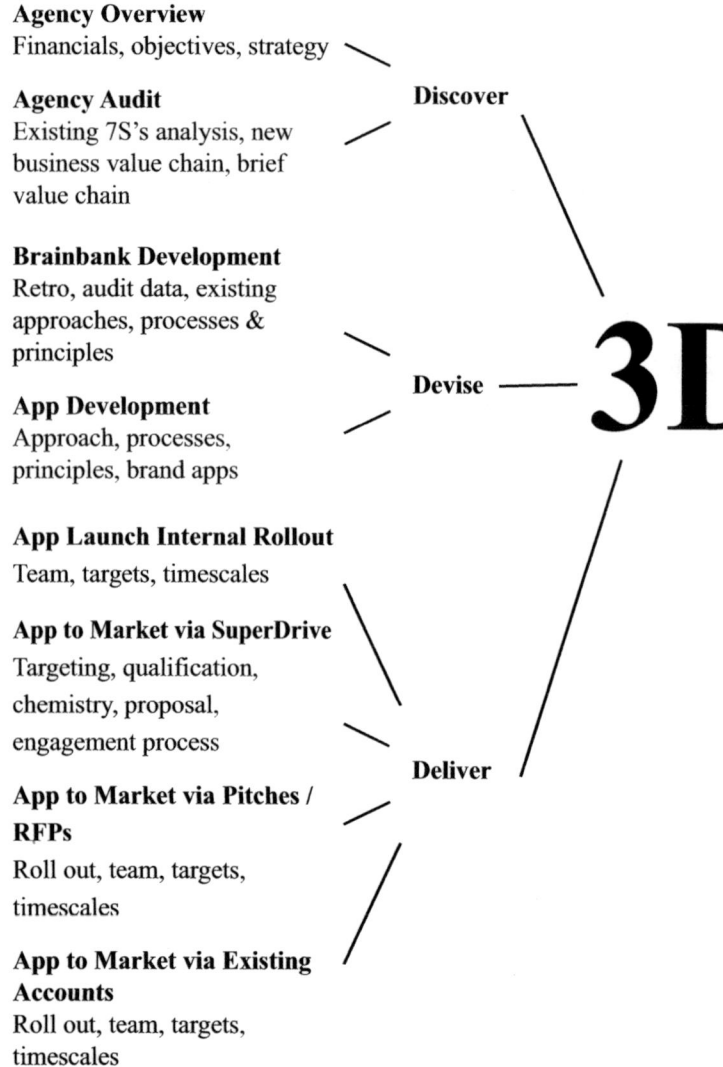

Agency Overview
Financials, objectives, strategy

Agency Audit
Existing 7S's analysis, new
business value chain, brief
value chain

Brainbank Development
Retro, audit data, existing
approaches, processes &
principles

App Development
Approach, processes,
principles, brand apps

App Launch Internal Rollout
Team, targets, timescales

App to Market via SuperDrive
Targeting, qualification,
chemistry, proposal,
engagement process

**App to Market via Pitches /
RFPs**
Roll out, team, targets,
timescales

**App to Market via Existing
Accounts**
Roll out, team, targets,
timescales

Discover

Devise ── **3D**

Deliver

Figure 19: The SuperDrive road map

NB. During the 'Deliver' stage it is useful to keep in mind that you'll constantly gain feedback from the market and should modify your proposition as appropriate. Keeping this in mind, it is advisable to swiftly and with a sense of urgency, create your apps, brand them and launch them to market. Don't pontificate. Don't ever think you'll reach your destination called 'perfection' – it's a continuous journey not a destination. The three following stages in the app development process may help create a framework to work to:

RIG   Rapid idea generation* > Construct the apps

RFG   Rapid feedback generation > Expose RIG to the market & listen intently

RMG   Rapid modification generation > Act upon RFG as appropriate

Sometimes also called rapid income generation depending upon the brief.

A guide regarding initial implementation timescales:

Discover 4 weeks

Devise   4 / 12 weeks depending upon existing internal resources

Deliver   RIG/RFG/RMG cycle approximately 14 weeks to run through the cycle

SUPERDRIVE ROI

See first 12 months as test, modify and perfect (set a lower financial target for the first year in order that the team smash it and have time to bed in new practices – say 30% of what we ultimately desire).

See second 12 months hitting 100% of desired target.

Notes